T0359113

"*Ovidiu Contras makes a valuable new contribution to the realm of process improvement. He uses his experience and creativity to open our eyes to the messiness of how people work together and make decisions in nearly all organizations. But more than that, Ovidiu guides readers to untangling the mess of everyday workplace interactions so that better progress can be made sooner and result in a more satisfying work experience.*"

Bob Emiliani, Award-winning author of
Better Thinking, Better Results

"*This is a wonderful book that in a simple manner allows all areas of a business to appreciate what Lean can do for them. This is powerful because it breaks the mindset that Lean is only good for production, showing it can be used from customer first contact, development, sales, all the way through to services.*"

Ralph Acs, President, Volvo Group Canada

"*Over the course of my new product development career, I realized that the technical part of the job was actually quite straightforward, with standard activities well defined and performed by well-intentioned and competent people. And yet we often had trouble to meet schedule and cost targets or to satisfy our customer' expectations. Why was that? Ovi's insight in his book is that the problems, issues and complexity are often associated with all the other things going on to support the activity flow, what he refers to as the information flow. It is this insight and his development of a methodology to apply VSM to recognize and reduce waste in the information flow that makes this book a must for those wishing to improve their business processes. The book is engaging and is full of real examples and practical tools to enable the reader.*"

Nick Perkins, Senior Director, Advanced
Product Development (Retired)

"*Based on real-life examples, this book takes VSM outside of the beaten tracks to reveal immaterial flow and make behaviors, organizational patterns and politics also visible. Ovi provides here a great cookbook on how to bring clarity, alignment and transformational results in complex environments dealing with intangible flows.*"

Matthieu Duhaime, President & COO, Avianor inc.

"For many, VSM is a tool for improvement facilitators, maybe managers. In reality, VSM is a powerful Leadership tool, exposing barriers, whether in process, transactions, office politics, etc. And this is precisely where Ovi's book delivers: it is simply full of examples and insights in almost every page, expertly blending theory with experience, in a context of high complexity. It is a work that, for me, opens the eyes into how VSM can probe into so many aspects of an organization and provide solutions, hence its considerable value in the body of VSM work today!"

Patrick Ross, Former Executive, Bosch Australia

"My first exposure to Lean was in 2006 when Ovi facilitated my first kaizen, and from that day on I was hooked. The way of looking into flow and waste to generate value is something that literally can change the game in a very significant way, especially in complicated environments. This book is a valuable guide for this matter. Ovi has been my sensei for all these years and I highly recommend his work."

André Desroches, Vice-president Operations, Pelican International

"The world is complex, and growing more complex Every day. Ovi has a unique ability to break down our 'tangled' world, and organize it in ways that uncover waste and help establish a clear path of removing it. From my new product development experience, I relate very well to the case studies presented in this book. They are far from being theoretical, they are illustrating what's really happening in the real world, and that's an extra benefit. I highly recommend Ovi's book to both professionals and leadership."

Pierre Harter, Director Research and Development, National Institute for Aviation Research (NIAR) at Wichita State University

"In his book, Ovidiu has provided real life examples of actions to avoid and identified opportunities for enterprises to make the most of their transition to Lean. He highlights common traps companies tend to make while transitioning to a new work model and explains how to make transformational changes to the organization that will last. Bringing humor and insightful comments, the book is simply a joy to read!"

Steve Tessier, Director, Shared Platform & Development Services (SPDS)

Untangling with
Value Stream Mapping

Untangling with Value Stream Mapping

How to Use VSM to Address Behavioral and Cultural Patterns and Quantify Waste in Multifunctional and Nonrepetitive Work Environments

Ovidiu Contras

Foreword by Art Byrne

Routledge
Taylor & Francis Group

A PRODUCTIVITY PRESS BOOK

First Published 2022
by Routledge
605 Third Avenue, New York, NY 10158

and by Routledge
2 Park Square, Milton Park, Abingdon, Oxon, OX14 4RN

Routledge is an imprint of the Taylor & Francis Group, an informa business

© 2022 Ovidiu Contras

The right of Ovidiu Contras to be identified as author of this work has been asserted by him in accordance with sections 77 and 78 of the Copyright, Designs and Patents Act 1988.

All rights reserved. No part of this book may be reprinted or reproduced or utilised in any form or by any electronic, mechanical, or other means, now known or hereafter invented, including photocopying and recording, or in any information storage or retrieval system, without permission in writing from the publishers.

Trademark notice: Product or corporate names may be trademarks or registered trademarks, and are used only for identification and explanation without intent to infringe.

ISBN: 978-0-367-51187-6 (hbk)
ISBN: 978-0-367-50566-0 (pbk)
ISBN: 978-1-003-05037-7 (ebk)

DOI: 10.4324/9781003050377

Typeset in Garamond
by Apex CoVantage, LLC

To Diana, Luca and Marco and to all the people that supported me throughout my career – you know who you are.

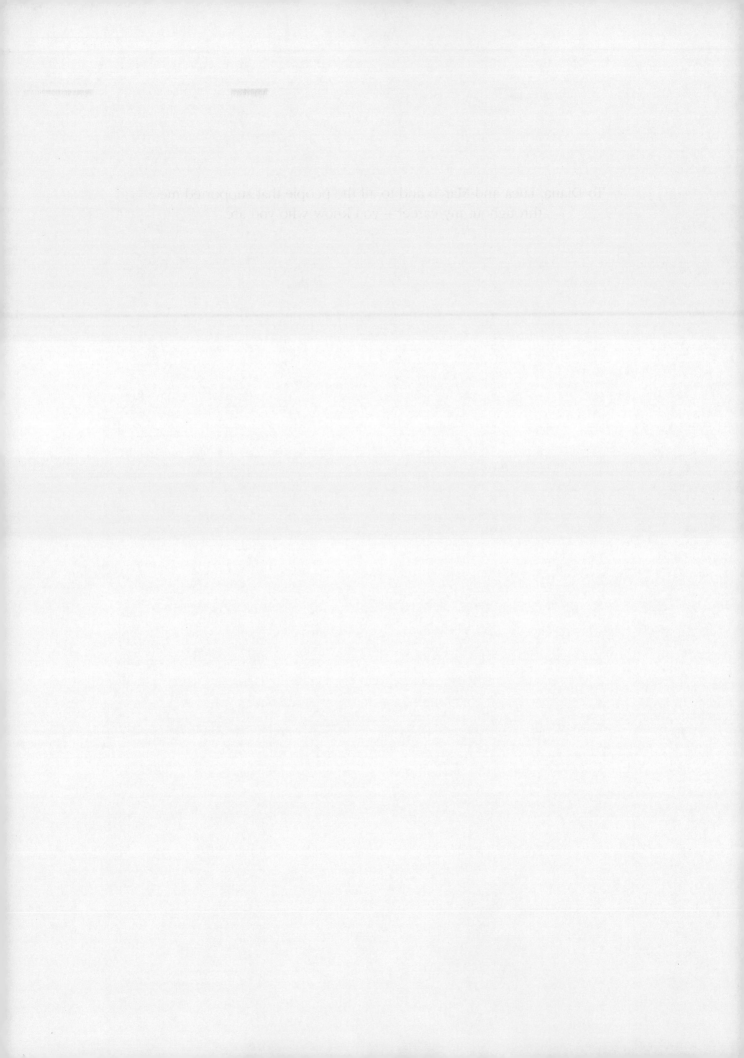

Contents

Foreword

Most companies that start down the Lean path, say 85% of them, view Lean primarily as a cost reduction program. They have heard that other companies have gotten significant cost reductions as a result of their Lean efforts and want to do the same, as they are constantly looking for productivity gains. They usually delegate this to their Vice President of Operations, as they see it as primarily a "manufacturing thing." They can't understand how it could possibly apply to other parts of the business, so operations will implement Lean while the rest of the company will stay in its traditional batch mode. This, of course, just sets up a lot of internal conflicts going forward as the Lean or flow part of the business and the traditional batch part are almost exact opposites in structure, culture and how things get done.

The fact that Lean is really a strategy and not a cost-reduction program is totally misunderstood by most companies. Think of it as a strategic way to run any type of business. The Lean focus is always the same: how to deliver more value to your customers than your competitors can. The methodology is very straightforward: remove the waste from your own operations in order to be able to deliver more value to the customer. When you remove waste, the time it takes to do anything is drastically reduced. Cost will be reduced as well, but this is a secondary factor to delivering more value to the customer. As a result, you can think about Lean as "a time-based growth strategy" where the market share gains from shorter lead time and faster response far outweigh the cost reductions that will also occur.

Now, "go forth and remove the waste" is easy to say but much harder to do. People get used to their current state and can walk by massive waste every day and never recognize it. For example, let's say your factory has a lot of mostly automated machines, each of which has its own operator. When you walk through the plant, the fact that these operators spend 80%+ of their day standing there watching the machine do its work doesn't seem wasteful to you. It is just the way it is. Now if you go home and watch your spouse load up the washing machine with clothes and then pull up a chair and sit there for the next 45 minutes watching the clothes go round and round, that may seem wasteful to you. At least it will seem odd, but the same thing in your factory will just seem normal.

To overcome this mindset, there are a lot of Lean "tools" that have been developed over the years, starting with Toyota and the Toyota Production System. Many of these apply specifically to the shop floor and are easy to use in environments where you can physically see what is happening. The four Lean fundamentals of (1) work to takt time, (2) one-piece flow, (3) standard work and (4) pull system, of course, drive everything we are trying to accomplish with Lean. They can be easily understood on the shop floor. But what about other parts of the business, like product development, accounting, inside sales, engineering, information technology, human resources? For most of these, you can't see any flow; there is no standard work; the concept of takt time doesn't exist, and all work is pushed not pulled to completion.

To deal with these situations, the Lean company uses a tool called value stream mapping or VSM. This is a pretty straightforward methodology to map the steps in a process, along with the elapsed time that it takes to complete the work. Usually, it is applied to fairly simple processes like order entry, the time it takes a loan application at a bank to go from start to finish or the steps needed to process accounts payable. There are lots of good books on the subject of VSM for these types of situations. But now with this book, *Untangling with Value Stream Mapping*, Ovidiu Contras has taken VSM into incredibly complicated processes that most people would say are impossible to fix. You can't see them; they are nonrepetitive; they exist in multifunctional environments; they have political and cultural barriers; and the waste is completely hidden.

Does any of this sound familiar? Do you want to know how to fix it and deliver more value to your customers? Well, hold on to your hats; you will be amazed at how Ovi uses very complicated examples to show you how to map the actual processes and not only eliminate the waste but also create a sustainable approach despite having many narrow functional departments having to buy into both the VSM process and the solutions.

Untangling with Value Stream Mapping takes us step by step to define the context of the problem, the ownership, the objective, the alignment of company politics and what is needed to get the commitment for success. The author uses real-life examples and explains the need for a champion and an owner of the process. He outlines the need for detailed up-front analysis and planning, including an initial value steam walk to outline the process. He shows us the need to divide the VSM into information flows, activity flows and time frames and does an exceptional job of showing what icons can be used to simplify an otherwise very complicated process.

I believe that *Untangling with Value Stream Mapping* makes a very valuable contribution to the Lean community, as it shows us how to use VSM to break down extremely complicated processes and be able to streamline them and remove the waste. I highly recommend this book to any company and management team that has complicated processes that until now you felt were impossible to improve. Buy the book; you will be amazed.

Art Byrne

Art Byrne started his Lean journey in January of 1982 during his first general manager role at the General Electric Company. He then went on to introduce the Toyota Production System to the Danaher Corporation from his role as Danaher Group Executive. As CEO of the Wiremold Company, he increased the company's enterprise value by just under 2,500% over the course of nine-plus years. He is the author of two books, The Lean Turnaround *and* The Lean Turnaround Action Guide. *He has won two Shingo Prizes and is a member of the* Industry Week Magazine *manufacturing hall of fame, the American Manufacturing Excellence hall of fame and The Shingo Academy (their version of a hall of fame).*

Acknowledgments

This book is made possible by:

The hard work of the teams I've been involved with – too many to be mentioned here – during numerous years, by preparing for the workshops, by contributing to the workshops, by making the changes decided in workshops, by sustaining the changes. The lessons learned from these experiences are the foundation of the book.

The change leaders who got involved and trusted me to train, coach and facilitate their teams: Alain Rousseau, Alexander Preis, Andre Desroches, Brigitte Lariviere, Claude Prairie, Dan Stewart, Daniel Lamarre, Dave Barrow, Derek Whitworth, Eric Filion, Fernando Ribeiro, Jim Sykes, Matthieu Duhaime, Nick Perkins, Pierre Harter, Ralph Acs, Richard Holland, Rob May, Sean Johnson, Steve Tessier, Suzanne Bernard, Tony Curry … and the list can go on.

The ones who shaped my career as a Lean practitioner: Art Byrne, Marypat Cooper, Rich Levesque.

The ones challenging conventional thinking about new product development, helping me to better understand how Lean applies in this field: Michael Kennedy, Brian Kennedy, Norbert Majerus, Lean Product and Process Development Exchange (LPPDE) conference.

The ones who helped me better understand classical management and the human side of Lean: Bob Emiliani, Patrick Ross.

The valuable suggestions from the reviewers: Alexander Preis, Brian Kennedy, Brigitte Lariviere, Michael Kennedy, Nick Perkins, Patrick Ross, Rob May.

Special thanks to Art Byrne for the foreword, to Nick Perkins for all the mentoring and the experimentation and to Michael Sinocchi for believing in this book.

Author Biography

Ovidiu Contras (*Ovi*) is a Lean coach and author of *Navigating the Lean Transformation*, a book covering some of his personal experiences in Lean transformation efforts as a continuous improvement employee, not as an external consultant.

His career started as a design engineer for high-temperatures industrial equipment. Since 2000, he has been actively involved in Lean transformation efforts as a Lean black belt, continuous improvement manager, kaizen promotion officer or Lean coach. Ovi's experience covers all the business aspects, from developing new products to servicing them, including the support functions like finance, IT, human resources, working for companies in aerospace, consumer goods and research and development. Ovi is specialized in the application of Lean principles in complicated multifunctional environments where the product is hard to see, and the work is nonrepetitive.

Ovi graduated as an engineer and studied graphic arts after graduation.

Introduction

It happened when the yearly employee survey had just come out. Among others, communication seemed to be a pain point.

We were a new team made up of people with very diverse backgrounds, diverse levels of experience, with a newly appointed manager and with an ambitious business goal in front of us. Our manager was determined to do something about the communication problem, so it was decided to fit a 5 Whys root cause analysis session into the next staff meeting, with me as a facilitator.

We started by working on the problem statement and with an introduction to 5 Whys, then, when we started the 5 Whys tree, the time allotted expired. Conclusion? We need another session! Invites went out, but because we were all busy working toward the ambitious business goal, we couldn't find common free time slots immediately but in about two weeks.

This pattern repeated several times because of the differences in perceptions and some lack of discipline. This greatly frustrated our manager, who then asked for more detailed guidelines on 5 Whys, which I developed in parallel with the sessions. After chasing our tails for a period, we eventually ended up with an action plan that was then implemented. Bottom line: it took us 43 calendar days to have an action plan, with only 5.5 hours of actual work, but with five reschedules.

How is it possible to remember all of this after so many years? While self-reflecting on what happened, I wanted to visualize the whole story from the beginning to the end, so I drew a value stream map (see the following picture). All I needed to do now was to glance over it and write the story – *please look at the picture, see if you can follow the narration.*

I have been using value stream mapping (VSM) since the beginning of my continuous improvement career, more than 20 years ago, but this time it was different: the product that I was after was not a physical part or a clear transaction like releasing purchase orders but something more intangible – an action plan, the result of a problem-solving exercise. Despite that, I was sticking to the essence of a VSM, making sure there's an activity flow (black ink), an information flow (red ink) and a time line.

Several things went through my mind while I was mapping: how do I capture the work done in parallel? How do I capture the decisions made

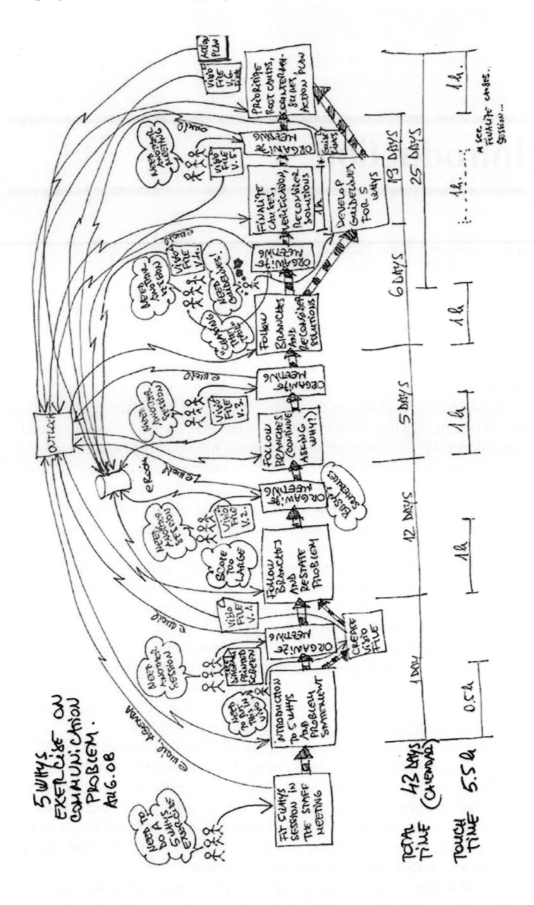

and their consequences? How do I capture the issues we were facing? How do I capture the manager's frustration? *Look at the picture – can you find how these questions were answered on the map?*

While drawing the map, I realized that in this case, by the nature of the work to be done, a value stream map is not about data boxes with cycle times, changeover times or efficiencies, value-added or non-value-added activities but about how people interact and work together, about how decisions are being made, about the struggles and issues popping up; they all have a tremendous impact on the end result. And then it hit me: all these things happen mostly in the information flow! And because I couldn't find anything in the current mapping methodologies, I started using people icons in red ink to illustrate the fact that people are part of the information flow and their decisions become triggers for doing work, using clouds to illustrate the issues, using people with dark clouds above to illustrate frustration.

I still remember my colleagues' reaction as I was showing them the picture; they were all smiling and totally relating to the map, saying, "Yes, that was a struggle." "That's exactly how I felt." Since that day, the way I've performed VSM exercises changed forever, for the biggest benefit of the teams that I coached and facilitated.

There's no bigger reward than seeing team members' reaction in front of the developing map, when pennies start dropping and you hear, "Wow, I didn't see it this way"; "now I know why we struggle so much"; "this is what I was saying for a long period of time, but no one listens – so great to visualize it!" So, what you have in your hands is the result of years and years of performing these types of exercises, adjusting along the way and incorporating lessons learned.

This book is based on the premise, "All models are wrong, but some are useful," per George E. P. Box. It helps people working in a tangled environment to build a useful model where they can recognize their work; they can recognize their environment; they can recognize their daily struggles and then translate their understanding of what's going on into another model that highlights the required improvements. In other words, it gives people working in a tangled environment the means to design a better world for themselves and their company. More about what's a tangled environment in Chapter 1.

Following this idea, this book describes all the required stages to go through a successful VSM exercise, starting with the preparation (Chapter 2), then mapping the current state and identifying waste (Chapters 3 and 4) and then mapping the future state and validating (Chapters 5 and 6). It ends with some results from performing VSM exercises in the conclusion. Fictional stories reflecting real-life cases are used to increase the reader's comprehension, and you have a summary of these stories in Appendix G. As you will surely notice, this book is not just about mapping but also about the main ingredients for achieving significant and sustained business benefits:

what it takes to prepare for major changes (Chapter 2), how waste is affecting work and how to deal with it (Chapters 4 and 5) and what makes major change sustainable (Chapter 6 and Conclusion).

What you'll find interesting in this book is the wide variety of topics, ranging from office politics, people engagement and commitment to change, technical ways to enable flow, to detailed instructions on how to map. They all complement each other to give you the best guide for streamlining tangled environments.

Do you struggle with VSM in multifunction environments where the product is hard to see and the work is nonrepetitive? Do you have trouble quantifying waste in this environment? Do you have trouble making office politics and behaviors visible? Do you want to engage stakeholders – including leadership – in making changes? Do you want to have significant and sustainable business benefits from your improvement activities? If the answer is yes to any of these questions, then this book is for you. Enjoy!

Chapter 1

How Can We Improve It if We Can't See It?

Denise had a blank stare on her face. She had trouble acknowledging what Louis was telling her: "It's really bad ... the survey results came out and show that people are not using the software." Louis added: "This adds to the fact that it took us three times longer and two times more money than originally budgeted."

After a long pause, Denise started whispering, "All this wasted effort ... all this money thrown out the window."

Claire just hung up the phone. It was a short call from one of the suppliers she was responsible for. The voice from the other side of the line was still echoing in her ears: "Claire, you must understand that we cannot ship you more parts if you don't resolve the unpaid invoices issue."

Worries and frustration started to pop up in her mind: "What am I going to do? There's no other reliable source for these parts! How come we didn't pay them??"

Frank could barely hear Ted's trembling voice: "The safety assessment people sent us the analysis results ... it's a fail ... the only way out is to drastically change the geometry ... we got the confirmation and have all the numbers ... this is big!"

Frank's face turned red: "Do you realize what you're telling me??" Then he blasted: "How am I going to tell the supplier we've changed the component design again? They have already machined the mold! Do you really want me to tell them to scrap it after spending all that money?? You guys just don't know what you're doing!"

What do Denise, Louis, Claire, Ted and Frank have in common? It is very apparent that they face difficult situations, but in order to nail the commonality, we need to hear their stories.

DOI: 10.4324/9781003050377-1

1.1 What's a Tangled Environment?

Denise, Vice President information technology (IT), and Louis, Engineering Process and Tools Director, are both working for a multinational company that develops and manufactures complicated products. A couple of years ago, the company started a very ambitious IT project called eHOPE, with the objective of integrating the Enterprise Resource Planning (ERP) system with the multi-platform software suite for computer-aided design and with a set of Product Lifecycle Management (PLM) products in order to streamline the product development work. It was not a smooth ride. Besides the inherent technical complications, leadership and team member turnaround (Denise and Louis were not a part of the original team), the project was haunted by scope changes and overlapping roles and responsibilities. More than a dozen IT, engineering and business functions were involved, like IT project office, data management, process and tools, design engineering, while working with the software provider and the solution architect. One source of frustration along the way was the difference of opinions from the different stakeholders on how to proceed. As stakeholders were defending their particular points of view, progress was slow and misguided, ending with late delivery and user frustration, as the delivered functionality didn't meet their needs.

Claire is a Supplier Account Manager, working in supply chain for another multinational company that uses a sophisticated ERP system to control production, inventories and accounts payable. This complicated system consists of three integrated main modules: one for finance, one for supply chain and one for production, with user access granted just for the corresponding function. Automated transactions are mixed with manual entries made by hundreds of people for thousands of suppliers. The inherent complications of the system make it such that the main stakeholders have just a partial view – their function's view – on the stream that links ordering a part, receiving the part, receiving the invoice and finally paying the invoice. In order to see what's happening with the unpaid invoices, Claire needs to navigate through several system transactions and scrutinize dozens of system screens and still might not be able to have the whole information. It might take her dozens of email exchanges or phone calls with production and finance people to finally understand what's wrong and why the supplier was not paid.

Ted, Engineering Director, and Frank, Program Director, are working together on a complicated new product development program for another multinational company. The inherent complications of the product make it such that several highly specialized engineering functions are required to interact with each other in order to progress the design, working with hundreds of requirements and design variables. Because they are developing a new product, they are in unexplored territory, dealing with unknowns, making assumptions and forced to go through a lot of iterations to solve the complicated design challenges. For example, one highly specialized engineering function gets data from another function, runs it through a specific model, performs analysis, applies engineering judgment, debugs the model and makes corrections – there could be several cycles like this – then hands on the resulting engineering data to another function, which then does the same. It goes without saying that this manual process allows for errors to go unnoticed and to propagate in the design. Additionally, people favor the designs that satisfy their narrow functional view, to the detriment of the product's view. In this environment, it is not uncommon to hear comments like, "I don't know what result I'll get, and I don't know when I'll give it to you," or "Our function's portion should be extracted and dealt with as separate … this is the only way we will get what our function wants in a reasonable time." Besides dealing with too many design variables, Ted's challenge is amplified by the fact that his team is dependent on all the other functions' work in order to perform properly while having no authority over the others, as they report to their own functional management.

Now let's take a step back and look at what kind of product they are dealing with: complicated IT solution for Denise and Louis, complicated system transactions for Claire, complicated new product design for Ted and Frank. What do these different products have in common? First, they all need several stakeholders' interactions in order to be transformed. Second, they are not physical; they are hard to see, residing in sophisticated, large information systems. Third, transforming the product requires contextual work, which is not repetitive.

So, what do Denise, Louis, Claire, Ted and Frank have in common? They all work in a **multifunction environment with multiple interdependencies, where the product is hard to see, the work is not repetitive and the work advancement is tedious and convoluted** (see Figure 1.1). **We call this a tangled environment.** Working in this

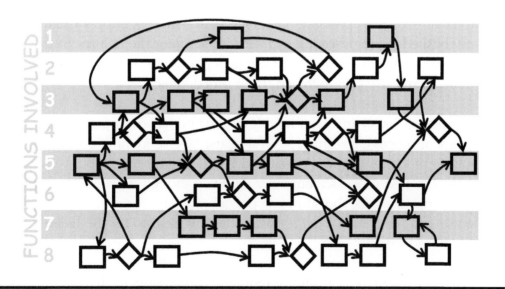

Figure 1.1 Typical Interactions in the Tangled Environment.

environment has inherent consequences: unclear view of what the product or service is and who needs it, how this product or service reaches the one that pays for it, very low visibility for stakeholders on the overall product or service transformation. In this environment, the holistic view of the process gets lost, with each stakeholder's individual view prevailing. This becomes a source of conflicting interests that are hard to resolve, resulting in defects and delays that propagate along the chain with costly consequences. Denise and Louis are faced now with a possible write-off in the books due to underutilization of the IT solution; Claire is facing a possible line stop and delayed delivery due to missing parts; Ted and Frank are facing a possible program cost overrun and delays due to extra supplier work.

1.2 Why It's Hard to Significantly Improve Work in a Tangled Environment?

If we were to ask Denise, Louis, Claire, Ted and Frank if this is their first time facing this type of situation, they would readily admit that this is not the first time. They would probably tell you about the improvement initiatives they were involved with in the past concerning exactly the same issues. Then they would probably add how those initiatives proved to be ineffective. This should not be a surprise, as the multifunction tangled environment is fertile ground for confusion, miscommunication, misalignment and conflict. Claire recalls the last time she was involved in an improvement initiative related to unpaid invoices:

> "We weren't able to gather all the required parties at the same table … they all claimed their portion of the process was running smoothly, therefore their presence was not required. Besides that, they all had other pressing matters to deal with. So, Supply Chain established some procedures in order to counter the failures in the process, then handed them for implementation to the other functions. Result? No one followed these procedures."

Ted was previously involved in at least four initiatives targeting the product development process, spanning several years: "We've identified years ago that the holistic process view was missing, driving design rework, but we never got to the detailed process reengineering. Even though we went through several reorganizations, the silo view prevailed."

Denise and Louis mandated a postmortem workshop for the failed IT solution introduction:

> "We succeeded to have all the required participants in the room, but we realized very soon that the scars from the past were not healed

yet, people wouldn't even talk to each other. When we finally got over it, it took us a couple of hours just to figure out what was our product … imagine the confusion during the project execution!"

What makes it hard to improve work in a significant way in a tangled environment? Here are some factors:

Several stakeholders are required to transform the product. As we saw in the IT project example, there were more than a dozen functions involved, not including service providers. So, if we want to significantly improve the way the product is transformed, we need everyone's contribution because overall improvement is more than just the sum of local improvements. Gathering all the required functions for an improvement effort is not an easy task though – remember Claire and the attempt to fix the unpaid invoices issue?

Fragmented process ownership. Claire doesn't have ownership over the whole stream linking ordering a part, receiving the part, receiving the invoice and paying the invoice. Ted doesn't have ownership over the whole stream linking all the specialized engineering functions' activities. With fragmented process ownership, improvement activities are at risk for at least two reasons: first, it's hard to get all the required stakeholders at the same table (see the previous point), as no one owns the whole process, so there's no authority to make the improvement call. Second, not having an owner for the whole process makes it hard to execute and sustain the improvement ideas, even if we succeed in having all the required stakeholders at the same table.

Working with a hard-to-see product. When the product is not visible, it is difficult to assess its overall transformation stage, as opposed to physical products, where we can easily follow how the raw materials are transformed or assembled into a finished product. Claire has trouble seeing at what transformation stage the invoice is: was the product from the supplier received? Was the invoice received? Was the payment stuck with finance? If we're not aware of the transformation stages of the product, it is difficult to figure out where the waste is and what the failure modes are, limiting the improvement ideas. This in turn won't allow for achieving a significant improvement.

Contextual work. When the work is dependent on a specific context, the required activities adapt to the context and won't repeat case after case. Ted's team won't design the same product they are designing today; it is highly probable that the next product will have completely different requirements, so the activities they need to perform won't repeat. When Denise and Louis started discussing having the postmortem, not everybody agreed with the need: "Why do this? We won't work on the same solution again … we're just wasting our time." Ted remembers hearing in a previous improvement attempt: "We're not manufacturing here; we don't do repetitive work, each analysis is different, so … why do this?" It is hard to engage people in continuous improvement activities when they perform contextual work.

The improvement tools. Although improvement tools are universal, careful consideration needs to be taken when applying them in a tangled environment. The root causes for poor process performance in a tangled environment are not easily identifiable due to numerous process activities, their hidden interdependencies and the multitude of stakeholders involved. The same applies to waste identification. For example, in Ted's environment, design iterations are not necessarily rework; they are required to gain more understanding or to optimize. Trying to remove design iterations works against acquiring the necessary knowledge and will end up in a defective or unoptimized design. Caution needs to be applied when using improvement tools in this environment because improper identification of root causes and waste won't allow achieving a significant improvement and, in some cases, can even hurt the performance.

1.3 Can VSM Help?

Making the overall process visible is the first step in understanding where the waste is and where the failure modes occur. This is paramount for the tangled environment, where lack of visibility is omnipresent: unclear view of what the product (or the service) is and who needs it, how this product (or service) contributes to the one the customer pays for, very low visibility for stakeholders on the overall product (or service) transformation. VSM is a specifically designed improvement tool* for making the process visible in order to identify waste and failure modes.

"Whenever there is a product or service for a customer, there is a value stream. The challenge lies in seeing it"; these are the opening words in the groundbreaking book *Learning to See*[1] where the VSM approach was exposed worldwide for the first time. This quote is meaningful to all environments, but in the case of tangled environments, it has even more meaning because the challenge of seeing the value stream is much bigger – for all the reasons mentioned in the previous paragraphs.

Learning to See details the VSM application in a mass production, manufacturing environment. Since then, other books were written to extend its use to the complete enterprise, including product development and more generic office work. Caution is required though when applying VSM in a tangled environment. Ted recalls, "During a previous improvement initiative we started value stream mapping the new product development process. As we were mapping the activities, we realized that we were reproducing what we had in our standards … nothing insightful came out. After a couple of hours, we abandoned …"

To understand the subtleties of using VSM in a tangled environment, let's see what a VSM is and why it's useful.

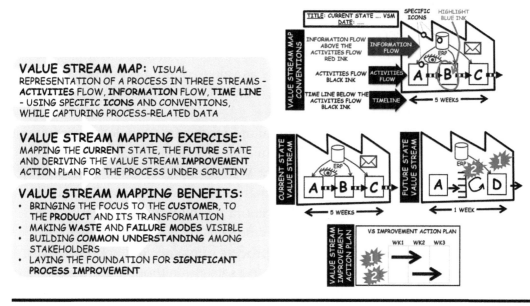

Figure 1.2 One-Pager VSM.

A value stream map is a visual representation of the process in three streams – activities flow, information flow and time line – using specific icons and conventions – activity boxes, push arrows, information path arrows, check, data manipulation – while capturing related process data. A VSM exercise consists of mapping the current state, mapping the future state and deriving the improvement action plan for the process under scrutiny. It is a diagnosis and communication tool while setting the stage for a structured plan to significantly improve the process (see Figure 1.2).

The VSM benefits can be summarized, but are not restrained to, as follows:

- Bringing the focus to the customer, to the product (or the service) and its transformation
- Making waste and failure modes visible
- Building common understanding among stakeholders
- Laying the foundation for significant process improvements

The work in a tangled environment can benefit from VSM too if we make an adjustment to existing approaches. Why do we need an adjustment? Because by focusing on the activities flow, they don't allow a fair capture of the sources of waste. Be it high-volume, low-mix manufacturing; low-volume, high-mix manufacturing; product development; or office, they all have a detailed focus on the activities flow and a more diluted focus on the information flow. For example, detailed activity data boxes call for values regarding cycle times, changeover time, uptime, availability, efficiency – which assume repetitive work patterns. This becomes an issue in tangled environments where the work is nonrepetitive. Additionally, this detailed focus on the activities flow limits the identification of waste and failure modes, as we saw in Ted's experience with VSM when the mapped activities were reproducing the activities in the standard process with no valuable insight. Some approaches call for labeling the activities as value-added, non-value-added or waste. This can be misleading too, as we saw in Ted's case, with design iterations not being wasteful activities.

As we previously stated, waste and failure modes in a tangled environment originate in behavioral aspects like confusion, miscommunication, misalignment and conflict, which current VSM approaches don't capture well. So, we need to focus more on the information flow and find ways to capture them there, as confusion, miscommunication, misalignment and conflict do not belong in the activities flow, but they need to be captured anyway, as they have a tremendous impact on the process outcome. Ted acknowledges, "The trouble doesn't lie in the design process itself – although granted, it could be improved – but in how and what information is feeding it."

In conclusion, VSM can definitely help improve work in tangled environments, with one condition: shifting the focus to the information flow, making sure its richness is well reflected in the map. Proper capture of the information flow allows going beyond waste and failure modes identification, by making behavioral patterns and organizational politics visible. The information flow helps tell the story, and we'll learn how to put it to work in Chapter 3.

You can find a summary of Denise's, Louis's, Claire's, Ted's and Frank's stories in Appendix G.

*NOTE: A value stream map, be it current or future state, does not fix anything; the **execution** of the value stream improvement action plan does.

Note

1 Rother, M., & Shook, J. (2003). *Learning to see: Value stream mapping to add value and eliminate MUDA.* ISBN-13: 978-0966784305, ISBN-10: 0966784308.

Chapter 2

Do We Really Know What We're After?

The more we navigate in a tangled environment trying to improve work, the more we realize how interconnected things are. The more questions we ask about ownership, the more complicated it gets, with "it depends" being one of the most popular answers. At the same time, we realize how unaware people are of what's happening outside of their part of the process. It's like the parable of the blind men and the elephant (see Figure 2.1), when a group of blind men inspect an animal they didn't see before and form their opinion on what that animal is by touching it. According to the part they touch, their opinion is made: the one touching the leg thinks it's like a tree trunk, the one touching the ear thinks it's like a fan, the one touching the trunk thinks it's like a snake …

Figure 2.1   The Blind Men and the Elephant.

DOI: 10.4324/9781003050377-2

2.1 Anyone Caring?

Like the blind men expressing their view of the elephant part they are touching, the stakeholders in a tangled environment see and understand just the part of the process they touch, with their improvement ambition limited to that view (see Figure 2.2).

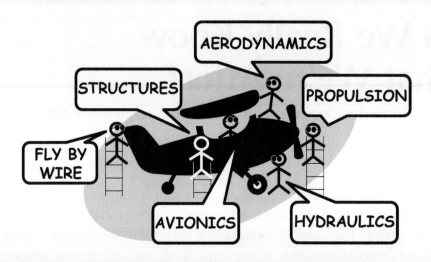

Figure 2.2   Ownership/Focus in the Aerospace Environment.

So, before even thinking VSM in this environment, there's some important work to be done. "There was no preparation," remembers Ted. "We just called a person familiar with facilitating VSM in operations, we got a short training, then we jumped at mapping the product development process … nothing insightful came out." Jumping directly into a VSM exercise without knowing the context, without a good idea of what the product is, without up-front commitment to improvement, without ownership, without all stakeholders involved and without knowing what problem we are trying to solve significantly reduces the ability to succeed. Good preparation is key to success.

Good preparation starts by figuring out what's the *business pain*, who's the *owner* and who's the *champion*. The business pain is something that hurts the business, typically related to low customer satisfaction levels or to poor business performance (very long lead times, not delivering on time, high prices, poor quality, high costs, poor service, etc.). Sometimes it's hard to pinpoint it. "I was not in a position to clarify the business pain," says Claire. "Is it related to the extra effort required, including expediting fees, to cope with shortages? … or is it related to frustrated suppliers who can initiate legal actions or can re-negotiate contracts at our disadvantage? … or is it related to frustrated customers who are asking for penalties and spread the word about our bad performance?" It takes someone who's position in the organization allows for clarification of the business pain. This person is the champion. The owner is someone who cares and is motivated to do something about the business pain, without necessarily owning the whole process. This gap is covered by the champion, who supports the owner's improvement effort from a higher position in the organization. This higher position in the organization gives the champion the leverage to bring together all the required stakeholders. In the postmortem workshop for the failed IT project, Denise, as an IT VP, was in a good position to convince fellow VPs to support the postmortem and allow their people to participate. Unfortunately, that was not the case for Claire. Her efforts to bring the stakeholders together for the unpaid invoice's improvement effort were not successful despite caring and being motivated to do something about it. She's the typical case of an owner without a champion. Denise and Louis are typical cases of a champion and owner fulfilling their roles by leading the improvement effort.

A VSM exercise without a clear business pain and clear ownership leads at best to marginal improvements that are not sustained.

2.2 What's the Context?

Once we have figured out the business pain, who is the owner and the champion, we need to understand the context surrounding the business and the history of fixing the business pain, including current initiatives, both potentially having a major impact on the VSM effort. Understanding the context surrounding the business helps establish a sense of urgency or the lack thereof. "When the quarterly results came out, the hit we took with the IT project didn't go unnoticed," remembers Denise. "The CFO asked, 'What are we going to do, to avoid this from repeating?' That was helpful for leadership alignment."

"What I didn't know at that time, was that the finance people were in the middle of generating all the numbers to close the current fiscal year, besides being severely understaffed," remembers Claire. "No surprise I got no traction."

"We've included in our yearly business plan the improvement of the engineering change process," says Frank, the program director. "So when we started discussions about the VSM effort, management couldn't back off." Understanding the history of fixing the business pain is also important.

"Those who cannot learn from history are doomed to repeat it." This great quote from George Santayana reminds us of the importance of making the effort to learn from our past mistakes in order to avoid repeating them. This is the case with previous attempts to fix the business pain. Was the scope too big? Were the root causes identified? What were the solutions? How were they implemented? Were they sustained? Answering these questions will help differentiate the current improvement effort from previous efforts by considering past errors and translating them into better preparation and

execution. "While trying to negotiate with stakeholders, someone asked, '*So, what's going to be different this time?*'" says Frank.

> "That awkward moment made me think … so, we performed a post-mortem workshop to discover what was done in the past. To my surprise, there were six previous attempts to fix the engineering change process in the past nine years and while a lot of ideas were considered, few were implemented because of budget constraints or people availability. Learning this helped us push for upfront commitment."

Because of the fragmented ownership in a tangled environment, it is not uncommon to have scattered improvement initiatives trying to deal independently with the same business pain at the same time. "While preparing for the VSM exercise," says Ted, "when we noticed that our key resources were excessively booked in meetings dealing with a closely related subject, we realized there's another initiative led by another specialized engineering function targeting model accuracy." Learning about current efforts targeting the same business pain helps consolidate resources and stop duplication of effort.

The business context and the current or past attempts at fixing the business pain provide priceless learning of the businesses' appetite for improvement, of lessons learned and effort consolidation; they have a strategic value when preparing a VSM exercise.

2.3 Trouble Engaging People?

The tangled environment has additional complications coming from the organizational structure. As we saw in Ted's example, the stakeholders touching the product belong to different groups, each having its own organizational structure (see Figure 2.3). As these groups report to several

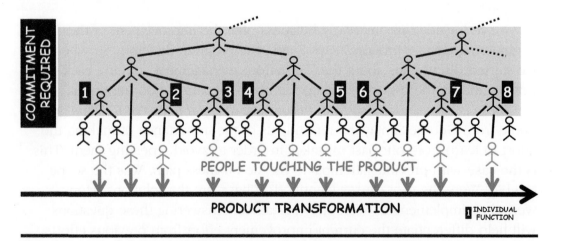

Figure 2.3 Functional Reporting Structure and Required Commitment.

directors and several VPs, it is mandatory to get alignment and commitment from all of them before the improvement effort because they are the ones responsible for the results, the budgets and the priorities of their respective groups. Now here's where things can get whacky: the engagement level can widely vary from strongly engaged to not engaged at all, depending on each group's objectives, each director's or VP's leadership style. Claire remembers, "I was discussing with a group of executives about the necessity of a VSM exercise when two of them started smiling while saying, '*Of course, you know Claire, no one's against the virtue, but you need to understand our reality ...*' and that was it ... everything stopped there." Additionally, organizational politics have a big impact, too. Hidden agendas, internal competition, backstabbing, manipulation, they all blossom in a tangled environment. The importance of understanding organizational politics is twofold: first, the influence over the engagement and, second, the influence over the information flow – more about the latter in Chapter 3. This becomes a problem because they all need to be equally engaged in order to achieve a significant improvement that is sustained. It takes extra effort from a champion and owner when they elaborate engagement strategies to figure out the political landscape: what are the personalities they must deal with, and what are the unwritten rules they need to comply with? In all circumstances, looking after the best interest of the company must be the leading thread.

"There were about seven directors owning different parts of the engineering change process," says Frank. "It took targeted one-on-ones, a lot of negotiation during a long period of time, but in the end, they all agreed to invest their people's time not just in participating, but in the implementation and sustainment of the improvements too. Having the VSM in the yearly business plan helped."

In parallel with managing the organizational alignment and commitment, a working team performs some preliminary work in preparation for the VSM under the guidance of a facilitator. The size of this team needs to be limited to a max of five or six people (including the owner and the facilitator), which means not all stakeholders will be represented, just the key ones. The advantage of a smaller group is that members can meet more frequently and can dedicate more time to gathering the necessary data. A smaller group makes sense economically too, as we don't want to invest too much into an effort at risk of being canceled if the required stakeholders are not on board. Canceling a VSM exercise is a definite option for the champion and the owner – it is better to cancel than to perform it without the required participation. "There was an initiative to streamline the testing part of the product development process," says Ted:

"We did a VSM without all the required people. The map was on a wall, then some – but not all – would come individually, as their time would allow it, and gave their inputs. Weeks went by until the current state was finished. When we finally had the opportunity to have all the required people together, strong disagreements about the content popped up … and persisted even after we left the conference room … everybody's time was wasted. What I learned later was the testing director has never bought into the idea of a significant improvement."

As leaders commit, they need to make sure the required people from their groups are freed up for the exercise and are fully engaged. This is not a trivial endeavor, as a VSM exercise could typically require more than three days for simpler processes. "It took us five days to map the current state VSM for the normal engineering change process," says Frank. "This shows the type of commitment we got from everybody to free up their people for such a long period of time." The list of the required participants is compiled by the small team to include them in communications related to the exercise once the commitment is achieved. Special attention should be paid to selecting the right members of the larger team – we must favor those who touch the product and have real insights, who properly represent the stakeholders.

Commitment and participation of all the required stakeholders is a go/no go for the VSM effort.

2.4 What Are We Trying to Fix?

The issues in tangled environments are usually the result of a multitude of causes coming from different parts of the process, so without proper scoping, we might end up fixing the wrong problem. As we said earlier, a business pain is something that hurts the business, is generic and has a larger scope, so in order to be more focused and get on the right track, we need to derive a problem statement from it. "The business pain was very clear: the write-off," says Denise.

> "But you can't do much about it if you stay at this level … so, after some thought we formulated a problem statement related to the bad quality delivered by the IT project, rationalizing that we'll catch the causes for lateness and for the busted budget at the same time."

"For us, the business pain was related to the delays in delivering new products," says Frank. "Everybody was complaining it takes forever to implement engineering changes … so, this translated into a problem statement detailing the long lead times between starting an engineering change and its implementation."

"The business pain was definitely related to the extra costs engaged with our suppliers," says Ted. "Then we derived a problem statement around the lateness of delivering mature requirements to the supplier, allowing us to catch the causes of non-validated assumptions and the inaccuracy of our models at the same time."

"When we finally got the engagement from everybody, I discussed with my champion, thinking that the problem statement is having shortages," says Claire.

> "But, during the discussion, it was apparent that the champion wanted to deal with the business pain of frustrated suppliers … so, the problem statement was formulated around suppliers not being paid, which was a scope down from my initial thoughts."

The easiest way to describe the relationship between the business pain and the problem statement is the subject in the problem statement is one of the many contributors to the business pain. This ensures a reasonable scope, effort-wise and time-wise, making sure we don't embark on some sort of "boiling the ocean" initiative. Bad quality delivered by the IT project is a contributor to the write-off. Long lead times for engineering changes are contributors to delays in delivering new products. Lateness in releasing mature requirements is a contributor to extra costs engaged with our suppliers. Suppliers not being paid is a contributor to shortages.

To be effective, the formulation of the problem statement needs to be factual and concise because the objective and the measure are directly related to it. The blurrier the problem statement, the blurrier the objective and the measure will be, leading to improvements that are neither significant nor sustained. Some data collection and analysis need to be done by the small team in order to support the formulation of the problem statement. "We started looking at credit holds for the past six months," says Claire.

> "Over twenty suppliers have put us on credit hold because they didn't receive our payment, and with about three times more suppliers, we were at credit hold risk because we passed the payment due date. *There are 87 suppliers that didn't receive their payment at the due date in the past six months* became the problem statement, with the derived objective of *100% on-time payments at due date, in three months from now,* and with the measure being *on-time payments to suppliers.*"

"Our small team started gathering data on lead times for the engineering changes," says Frank.

> "The numbers were all over the place, ranging from one month to over a year. We needed to make some sense of these numbers, so we rationalized the changes in simple, normal and complex, according to the work content. Once we did this, lead times aligned pretty well as they were dependent on the work content: more complex the change, more functions and people involved, more hours

required. *It takes 173 days for a normal engineering change to be implemented* became the problem statement, with the derived objective of *cut the lead time for a normal engineering change in half, in four months from now* and with the measure of *lead time for a normal engineering change.*"

"We did some digging and found documents related to the original scope and initial requirements for the IT project," says Louis, "then we formulated the problem statement: *The eHOPE IT project delivered less than 60% of the original business requirements, with less than 40% being actually used.* The objective: *New IT projects to meet 100% of the business requirements* with the measure: *business requirements met.*"

"What we found looking into the official documents exchanged with the supplier was mind-blowing," says Ted.

> "We've changed our requirements a dozen times, from which about half were major changes with big impact on supplier's work … so, the mature requirements were released 5 months later than scheduled … this led us to the problem statement: *Mature requirements for the critical component were released 5 months later than scheduled to the supplier,* with the derived objective: *On-time release of any new component requirements to suppliers, with no major changes after release* and the attached measures of *on-time delivery of requirements* and *major requirements change after release.*"

Factual and concise problem statements, derived from the business pain and linked with the objective and with the measure, are necessary to focus the improvement effort and achieve significant improvements that are sustained.

2.5 What's the Big Picture?

A common theme for tangled environments is the unclear view of what the product or the service is, along with stakeholders' blurred visibility on the overall product or service transformation and blurred visibility on how they contribute to what's delivered to the paying customer. "We started using the term *paying customer* because of our continuous improvement legacy," says Ted,

> "where everybody would be someone else's internal customer. This was generating a lot of confusion and was reinforcing our silo behaviors. So, we abolished the term internal customer and introduced the term paying customer to make sure everybody

understands who is buying our products, contributing to our salaries. In our environment we're far from the paying customer, so we have difficulty in relating our daily work to it, which is not good, because we all know happy customers make a good business."

In a tangled environment, there are a lot of people who don't work directly on the final product that gets delivered; they touch supporting subprocesses feeding it, so it is important to understand the product we touch and how this product feeds into the final product. This should be clarified by the small team before the VSM exercise, along with clarifying the product's main transformation stages, process starting and ending points and the link to the paying customer. This will allow everybody to have a high-level, holistic view and understand their contribution to the whole, not just to the local. As far as having difficulties visualizing the product, remember Denise's earlier remark? "It took us a couple of hours just to figure out what was our product." Her conclusion?

> "And that was time well spent! Here's what we've come up with: *our product is a process incorporating best practices, supported by tools and implementation procedures.* This definition alone helped enormously in realizing what went wrong during the project execution: because fixing the process became a nightmare, the focus shifted towards the easy stuff, like reconciling software & system architecture, so we ended up coding a bad process."

"The real challenge though," adds Louis,

> "was to make the link from our product to the paying customer. Let me explain: we deliver a process supported by tools, best practices and instructions to new product development teams, who will eventually use it to bring a new product to the market. Quite a stretch, no? What we realized while pushing the thought, is that by not delivering the required functionality, we contributed to the new product development process inefficiencies, translated into late delivery to the paying customer."

"For us, the easy part was defining what's the product," says Frank,

> *"a normal engineering change.* Then, we identified the main transformation stages: Initialization, technical analysis, financial analysis, implementation plan, sourcing validation, change validation, release to production, modified product. Although we already had process maps available, this was not an easy task, because of the conflicting inputs we got from the different stakeholders we consulted. Once

we converged, the link to the paying customer became apparent, as our engineering change transformed into a new or modified part being assembled in the final product that was delivered."

"We realized that our product is actually *requirements*," says Ted.

"True, we perform analysis, we size, we design, but in the end, we hand a set of requirements to our supplier, who, in turn, delivers the physical component. Our job is really making sure the component integrates well in the overall product design and is compliant with the overall product safety requirements. We stumbled though over the main transformation stages. Our work being highly iterative, we never know in advance how many iterations we need in order to get out mature requirements to the supplier. We churned for some time, until we've identified three main loops centered around the critical cases that the integrated component needed to be compliant with, so we settled for these transformation stages: *configuration compliant with criteria A, configuration compliant with criteria B, configuration compliant with criteria C, requirements*. Although any engineer can tell you this within seconds you ask the question, the churn we went through figuring this out was a good testimony of how focused on the small, detailed tasks we were. The link to the paying customer was blurred, too ... we made sure everybody understood how the immature requirements for the component contribute not just to extra costs, but to delivery delays for the final product, therefore impacting the paying customer, too."

"The product everybody agreed on is *payment to the supplier*," says Claire.

"And the related transformation stages were identified as ordering the part (artifact: purchase order), receiving the part (artifact: receiving bill), asking for payment (artifact: invoice) and paying (artifact: payment notice). Pretty simple, isn't it? But we realized how some of the stakeholders were not equally aware of their impact on the paying customer. The link between not paying suppliers – not having parts on the assembly line – late delivery seemed blurred, because their daily work was way upfront and not related to deliveries."

The VSM exercise could yield questionable results without the big picture sorted out beforehand. Figuring out what the product is clarifies what the product transformation stages are. Clarifying the product transformation stages becomes a verification point for the VSM – can we recognize the transformation stages on the map? Are all related artifacts captured on the map? Missing stages or artifacts on the map can be triggers for further investigation (did we miss anything?) or indicators of faulty execution (*oops, we jumped this stage*, or *we didn't use artifact x*). Caring about the paying customer is key; therefore, clarifying the link to the final product helps all involved realize how they contribute to it and at the same time how they contribute to customer satisfaction.

2.6 What Is It Like Being the Product?

Now it's time for the small team to see for themselves how the product is transformed from the beginning to the end at the actual workplace. Seeing how things get done and talking with the actual people who do the work is helpful for data gathering and understanding the work-related challenges. As they already know what the main transformation stages are, the starting and end points, the small team is ready to become the product and walk through the process, with the objective of making observations and gathering data and artifacts. There's some preparation required (see value stream walk preparation checklist – Appendix A) to establish the trajectory, the approximate duration for the walk and to make sure the required people are available. In a tangled environment, the most common answer to questions related to how we transform the product is "it depends." Using a real example will greatly help in getting clear answers, as people have a reference they can relate to. This real example needs to be documented in advance by looking into information systems for transactions and time stamps to recompose the transformation stages and the time line. This real example can be used to do the VSM exercise; that's why the criteria to choose it is important: *the example should be a typical case that is reflective of today's reality (not the best, nor the worst case), covering the process from the beginning till the end and with available time stamps for different transformation stages – especially for the start and the end.*

Walking the cross-functional process can be long and could take some time, as in tangled environments, people are typically grouped by function or department and sit in different areas or locations – maybe even different countries!

"As we became the normal engineering change EC3708," says Frank, "we walked the site, visiting scattered areas on different floors, including production, planning and engineering ... quite a spaghetti ... it took us half of a day to walk it all!"

"For us," says Claire, "walking the payment for the purchase order PO4435 involved driving to two other locations, one where parts were received and another one where the finance department was located."

Besides specific questions related to the real example, the team can use a checklist with generic questions (see the VS walk execution checklist) but should not forget that the main objective for asking the questions is learning, not making judgments or offering solutions. "As we were seeing people," says Frank,

> "they walked us through tons of information systems screens … others would pull out physical files out of their drawer to show us piles of printed email exchanges … when I asked *why are you keeping these?*, the person replied *just in case someone claims the information is stuck with me, so I have the proof it's not.* I was about to make a comment about this, but then I remembered I should not make any judgments."

"First thing we noticed when we arrived in the goods receiving area," says Claire,

> "was how clustered the place was, with piles of boxes all over the place. I was thinking *how can anyone work in a place like this?* Then, we saw the employee's back and forth: collecting the paperwork from the boxes, making data entries in the office, answering calls … someone even came in a rush asking for some parts … that made me think. When we finally get to talk, we learned that in the area there were about 5 days of received parts and the other receiving goods employee was sick for a couple of days. … I was glad I didn't express what was in my mind!"

"We arrived in the area of the first specialized engineering function, Failsafe," says Ted,

> "and noticed the team's board being overcrowded with tasks. Now, we understood the struggles this team goes through servicing several new product development programs, and why their priorities were not necessarily our priorities. I was tempted to suggest some improvements to their way of working, but then I realized this was not part of the walk, but part of the VSM exercise."

During the walk, process artifacts should be collected, like reports, transaction print screens, job aids – anything helpful to complete the picture of what happened. These will be used in the VSM exercise as facts and data, making the map a reflection of reality. "I wanted to collect the process map as an artifact," says Frank, "when the person that pulled it from the binder told me *no one really follows it, it's too restrictive* and *does not accommodate all the different cases we deal with.* I took it anyways, just to check if there's something to add to the main transformation stages."

The information gathered during the walk needs to be documented and made available to all the concerned parties. In some cases, it could be used

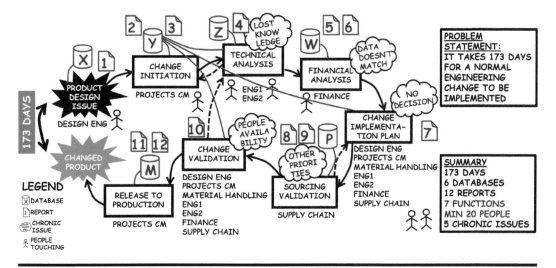

Figure 2.4   EC3708 Normal Engineering Change Walk.

as a call for action to engage those not totally bought in. "We took an 11 x 17 [inch] sheet of paper and sketched our trajectory," says Frank,

> "positioning the databases involved, the reports that were generated, the main issues and the different people touching EC3708 [see Figure 2.4]. We presented it to the stakeholders and after seeing it, they all agreed this is not acceptable and something has to be done to correct it. The report out from the value stream walk proved to be a very effective engagement tool."

The report out should include the problem statement backed with facts and data, the objective, the measure, the summary of the VS walk, along with the names and functions of the people from the bigger team who will perform the VSM exercise. This document is attached to the invitation that all the required participants receive for the VSM workshop.

The value stream walk is a necessary step in performing a VSM exercise to ensure no precious insights are overlooked, which might happen if we skip it. In the meantime, the walk ensures structured data and artifacts collection, providing the needed objectivity for a successful VSM exercise.

2.7 What's the Motivation?

As you've seen, preparing a VSM exercise is not an easy endeavor (see the VSM exercise preparation checklist – Appendix A). Starting with engagement and ending with data collection, all the steps build on each other and require time and a lot of effort. It's going to be difficult for an owner or a champion to keep up the pace without being highly motivated to pursue this. "I'm obsessed with eliminating waste," says Frank,

> "and throughout my career I found VSM to be an excellent vehicle for seeing and removing waste. It counts having good experiences with it though, especially in the type of environment we're in! The fact that I had an excellent VSM first experience helped me becoming an unconditional to it: We succeeded to improve from 0%, never meeting to 100%, always meeting the first critical milestone for custom design products."

"I knew VSM from my days in operations," says Denise, "but I never thought it can be used for an IT project, until I was exposed to an engineering VSM dealing with the same pain we went through ... that's when I said to myself, *we must try it!*"

"I heard of VSM from my employees with manufacturing experience," says Louis,

> "but didn't know much about it. ... I was familiar with all sorts of mapping methodologies, but not with this one. When Denise suggested we should perform a VSM exercise for our postmortem on the IT project, I became defensive *it might work for manufacturing, but not for this!!!* Then Denise brought me to see what the engineering folks did ... my jaws dropped, and my defensive attitude too."

"When Frank tried to convince me to perform a VSM exercise," says Ted,

> "my eyes rolled over: *look, I did this twice and that's enough, no more VSM, it simply doesn't work in this environment* ... then I told him about the new product development VSM tentative and about the testing VSM disaster. Without saying anything, he invited me to see what they were doing for the engineering change management process. While facing the map, I understood we approached it the wrong way in the past, then started to seriously think how I can make it work this time around."

"I was involved in an aftermarket VSM exercise in the past," says Claire,

> "when they were dealing with part shortages impacting the product servicing schedule. I was impressed by how the VSM unfolded all the waste and disconnects contributing to the issue, so it wasn't a big stretch for me to see how this type of approach could help us dealing with the unpaid suppliers' pain. When I finally had my champion, I didn't hesitate to share my previous VSM experience with her and we agreed to proceed with it."

There's no substitute for the work that the owner, the champion and the small team perform in order to prepare the VSM exercise. Understanding of what we're dealing with, ownership and dedication are the main ingredients to good preparation, positioning the VSM effort toward significant and sustained benefits.

Chapter 3

What's Important to See, and How Do We Capture It?

Finally! After a successful preparation involving a lot of effort, all the necessary stakeholders are committed and ready to contribute. It's time for the current state VSM (see current and future state checklist Appendix A3.).

3.1 Everybody on the Same Page?

The objective of the current state VSM is to have an accurate map that reflects reality, objectively mirroring what happened in the chosen example, thus setting a sound basis for waste, failure modes and behavioral patterns identification. It is performed by a larger team than the one doing the preparation work. This larger team must not exceed 12 to 15 members, for effectiveness reasons, but at the same time, it is very important to include all the stakeholders (sometimes it is possible to identify people experienced with several functions' work). The challenges raised by this type of exercise are related to rapidly growing the people's common understanding and with getting all the participants to actively contribute. With more people involved, more time is required to get on the same page, and there is less opportunity for individual contribution. The small team's level of understanding is higher than the larger teams'; it requires some time at the beginning of the exercise to make sure everybody understands why this effort is necessary and how it will be conducted. Here's where the material from the value stream walk report comes in handy: clarifying the business pain, the problem statement and the objective; clarifying what's the product and the product transformation stages; and clarifying how the product fits into the final product delivered to the paying customer. These clarifications help all participants to understand the objective of the exercise and the underlying problem to be solved, to realize how they contribute to the product and at

DOI: 10.4324/9781003050377-3

the same time how they contribute to customer satisfaction. This will put the larger team in the right mindset for a successful VSM exercise. A refresher on the real case is required too. This activity is usually conducted by the owner, introduced by the champion and can be part of a separate preliminary session before the actual mapping session.

As we saw in the previous chapter, the real example is very important to take ambiguity out, to avoid answers like "it depends," to objectively assess reality. Don't forget: the nature of a tangled environment allows for a lot of variation with regard to process execution. The danger of going generic in this type of exercise is to embark on endless circular discussions regarding all the possible execution paths. This is counterproductive and becomes an obstacle for progressing the mapping. There's a need for a common thread to focus the discussions; therefore, *the real case example is a must*. The team can use artifacts collected during the VS walk to make sure everybody relates to it.

Another important thing for the larger team to understand is what methodology will be followed. Even if some are familiar with VSM, it is always recommended to give a brief description of what a VSM exercise is (see "Can VSM Help?" and Figure 1.2, One-Pager VSM, in Chapter 1) and how it is performed.

Introducing the technique can be done with an example that everybody understands while explaining the mapping pattern, the mapping conventions and the icons used. This activity is usually performed by the facilitator (for more on this, please see the "Modify Drawing" example under the "What Does It Look Like?" section).

There are several means for doing the mapping: using software, using a whiteboard and markers, using paper, sticky notes and markers, and they all have advantages and disadvantages (see Table 3.1).

The decision on what means to use in the exercise belongs to the small team, which needs to consider how geographically spread out the required participants are, how well equipped with conference rooms the team is and the IT systems the organization is using, not forgetting that the main objective is to create a dynamic environment where everybody contributes, building *strong map ownership*. By building strong map ownership, I mean the process by which the participants make the map their own's. It's a gradual process, fueled by the common understanding of the holistic view that comes from everybody's active contribution (see Figure 3.1). With strong map ownership, people identify themselves in the map; they can recognize their daily struggles, therefore commit to the improvement, becoming advocates for the change. Without developing strong map ownership, it is extremely difficult to achieve significant improvements that are sustainable.

The following sections are particularly of interest for the VSM facilitators.

Table 3.1   Means of Doing the Mapping

Means of Doing the Mapping	Main Advantages	Main Disadvantages
Software, VSM specific or generic	• Facilitates participation from all over the world. • Easier reconfiguration of the map elements when the situation requires it. • Icons are readily available. • The writing is easy to understand. • No need for wall space or stationery. • The map can be immediately saved, stored and electronically shared.	• Less dynamic environment – one typing, all the rest watching, harder to make everybody contribute. • Weak map ownership. • It takes longer time to achieve common understanding. • Less visual impact when communicating. • Screen size limits the overall map visibility, the bigger the map, the less visible it is – need to go with partial views to see better. • Dependence on software, computer, projector and connectivity availability, connection quality, software-related skills of the one mapping.
Handwritten, whiteboard, paper, sticky notes, markers	• More dynamic environment – everyone can write in turn, easier to make everybody contribute. • Strong map ownership. • The common understanding is achieved faster. • Big visual impact when communicating. • Good overall map visibility. • Not dependent on software, computer, projector and connectivity availability, connection quality, software-related skills of the one mapping.	• Participants need to be in the same room, difficult to involve the ones participating over video or telephone. • Need wall space or a long whiteboard. • Difficult reconfiguration of the map elements when the situation requires it, less difficult when sticky notes are used. • Dependence on someone's writing skills to understand the writing. • Stationery required, less when a whiteboard is used. • Documenting the map through photos or through redrawing the map with software.

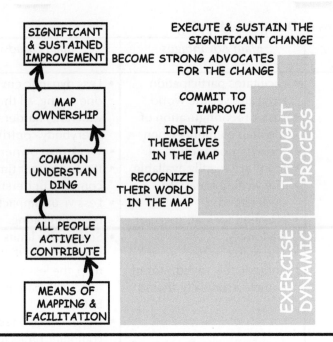

Figure 3.1   The Exercise Dynamic Influencing the Thought Process.

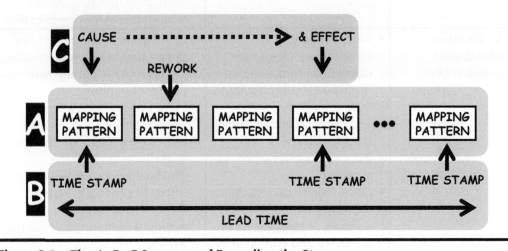

Figure 3.2   The A–B–C Sequence of Recording the Story.

3.2 Ready to Record?

Remember Ted's remark? *"The trouble doesn't lie in the design process itself – although granted, it could be improved – but in how and what information is feeding it."* Ted's point reflects the reality of a tangled environment, where waste and failure modes originate mostly in confusion, miscommunication, misalignment and conflict, coming from the use of scattered and numerous information systems, having different views and priorities, working with unreliable tools, proceeding with knowledge gaps and being motivated by organizational politics. These are very important things to be able to see, and they are unveiled with questions like the following: Where did the information come from? Who generated it? Was the information accurate or up to date? What were the assumptions surrounding the information? Was the processed information compatible with the processing means?

Was the right moment to process the information? Was the information shared? Who should have been made aware of the information? So, there's a need to record what happened in a way that facilitates the answers to these types of questions. We do this by using the mapping pattern (A), by adding time stamps and lead time (B), by adding rework and cause and effect elements (C) (see Figure 3.2).

3.2.1 The Mapping Pattern

The mapping pattern (A) is the sequence of constructing the map, a structured way of populating the activities and information flows, making sure that important elements that can reveal waste and failure modes are not left out. It's a consistent way to capture the story, facilitating the reading and the analysis once complete. The mapping pattern consists of activity – information – issues and is repeated until the map is complete. Here are some details about the components of the mapping pattern (see Figure 3.3):

■ Activity-related details (see Figure 3.3–1) include a short description, what function performs it, the activity touch time and the activity elapsed time. The touch time is the time of uninterrupted transformation of the activity, the time it takes for the activity when performed continuously, without interruption. The elapsed time is the time measured from receiving the signal to start work until the output is available for the next activity and includes the transformation time and the idle time.

■ Information-related details (see Figure 3.3–2) include trigger, input, output, enablers, and info out. The trigger is the signal that tells the person to start working on the activity. It could be an email, a discussion, an order, a workflow signal, a meeting. The input is what the activity transforms and includes details like input format and input source. For example,

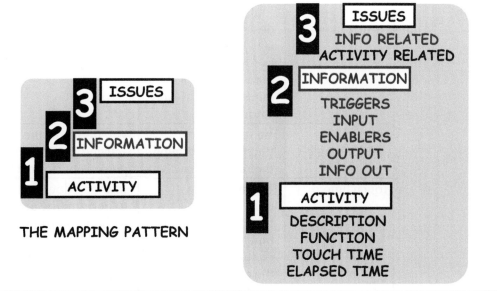

Figure 3.3 The Detailed Mapping Pattern.

if the activity is "Modify Drawing," the input is the current, not modified, version of the drawing and is a "*.catpart*" document that resides in ENOVIA. The output is the result of the transformation made by the activity. For the same example, the output is the modified version of the drawing, still a "*.catpart*" document that resides in ENOVIA but under a new revision name. The enablers are all the elements that influence how the activity is performed. Enablers could be documents like standards, work instructions – in which case the format and the source are recorded – or specialized software, or a means of performing the activity, like checking, manual manipulation of data. In the "Modify Drawing" example, one needs the CATIA software, needs to check and retrieve the current version of the drawing from ENOVIA, needs to check what's in the drawing and to manually modify it and then to save the modified version in ENOVIA. The info out is additional information generated by the activity, different than the output. For the previous example, it could be an email, a discussion, an update to a task list, all related to drawing modification.

■ Issues – related details (see Figure 3.3–3) include activity-related issues or information-related issues. The activity-related issues are specific to performing the activity. For the "Modify Drawing" example, the issue of "error messages" actually slows down the activity, delaying the transformation of the drawing. The information-related issues are particular to information feeding the activity. For the same example, the issue of "server down" prevents retrieving the drawing from ENOVIA, delaying the transformation of the drawing, while the issue of "wrong standard used" influences the quality of the modified drawing.

Table 3.2 Mapping Pattern Summary

Mapping Pattern Component	Subcomponent	Subcomponent Description	Questions
Activity	Activity description	Contains a brief description of the activity performed, two to five words max. It includes at the minimum a verb and a noun	What is the activity?
	Function performing it	The specialized function performing the respective activity	Who performs the activity? One or several persons perform it?
	Touch time	The time of uninterrupted transformation, the time it takes to continuously perform the activity without interruption	How long does it take to perform the activity without interruption?

(*Continued*)

Table 3.2 (*Continued*)   Mapping Pattern Summary

Mapping Pattern Component	Subcomponent	Subcomponent Description	Questions
	Elapsed time	Includes the transformation time and the idle time	How long does it take from the input for your activity to be available to someone to use your output?
Information	Trigger	The signal that tells the person to start working on the activity	How do we know when we need to start executing the activity? What's the signal to start performing this activity?
	Input	Whatever gets transformed by the activity	What does this activity transform? What's the format? Where does it reside?
	Output	The result of the transformation performed by the activity	What does this activity deliver? In what format? Where does it reside?
	Enablers	The enablers are all the elements that influence how the activity is performed and include documents, tools and means of performing the activity	What is needed in order to perform the activity? Where does it reside? In what format? What are we checking? What manipulation of data occurs? What workflow do we follow?
	Info out	Information generated by the activity other than the output	What other information other than the output does this activity generate or provide?
Issues	Activity	Issues related to the activity	What are the issues related to performing the activity?
	Information	Issues related to the information feeding the activity	What are the issues related to the information feeding the activity?

Table 3.2 summarizes the detailed mapping pattern components.

Once the sequence (A) is completed and the mapping patterns captured, the link between the activities needs to be made. As the activities could be performed in series or in parallel, the links need to clearly show the path between them. This is done using the "push" arrow (see "What Does It Look Like?") icon.

3.2.2 Time Stamps and Lead Time

<u>Time stamps and lead time</u> (B) are additional time-line elements; they can be captured as the map evolves or added at the end.

- Time stamps – recorded dates in information systems for certain transactions that can be correlated to performing specific activities and captured in the map below the corresponding activity.
- Lead time – is the total time of the process from start to end and is found through the time stamps. It is not unusual to get the start and end date from different information sources though; in tangled environments, it is rare to have data from start to end in one single place. It is captured when all the activities are on the map.

Sometimes it is not possible to assess the touch time or the elapsed time for certain activities, so it's ok not to have them on the map. The time stamps and the lead time are mandatory though; they need to be available during the preparation work (see "What Is Like, Being the Product?" in Chapter 2). Without them, the picture is incomplete. The lead time and the time intervals between time stamps can be expressed in what measure of time is appropriate (days, weeks, months, etc.), with the only rule to keep it consistent throughout the current and future state map. For example, if we capture the time intervals in calendar days, we will keep calendar days for all time intervals of the map; we won't mix them with working days.

3.2.3 Cause and Adverse Effect, Rework

<u>Cause and adverse effect, rework</u> (C) are elements in the information flow required to complete the picture:

- Cause and adverse effect – highlights the causal link between two activities (or information flow elements related to the two activities) usually separated by a long period of time, one being the visible cause and the other one being the adverse effect. For the "Modify Drawing" example, when after a long period of time another person using the modified drawing realizes it is incorrect (adverse effect), the highlighted link would be between the realization activity – for instance, "checking drawing" and the issue of "wrong standard used" (cause). The effect could trigger a rework or not. All recorded causes and adverse effects need to be compiled into a separate summary table, with a detailed description of the visible cause, of the adverse effect and of the impacts. They represent the recorded failure modes.
- Rework – highlights the moment when the need to redo the previously performed work is identified. For the "Modify Drawing" example, that

would correspond with the moment when the one that made the modification realizes that the standard was not the one that was supposed to be used or when another person using the modified drawing realizes that the drawing is incorrect. All recorded rework needs to be compiled into a separate summary table, with a detailed description of the rework and the impacts (see the example in Appendix D3).

The A – B – C sequence described earlier ensures that all the required elements telling the story of what happened are captured, making it easy to identify confusion, miscommunication, misalignment and conflict, along with behavioral patterns and organizational politics. Now, let's see how they are visually captured on the map.

3.3 What Does It Look Like?

3.3.1 Mapping Conventions and Icons

Making the story visible is achieved by using mapping conventions and icons. As a reminder, a value stream map consists of the activities flow, the information flow and the time line. The activities flow captures product transformation steps and who performs them. The information flow captures the information required to transform the product, the hard-to-see product itself in its different stages of transformation, the issues, the ways of working and the transformation-supporting means, the rework and the cause and effect relationships. The time line captures the transformation-related times. The basic mapping conventions include the following (see Figure 3.4):

■ Title and date at the top
■ Black ink for the activities flow and time line

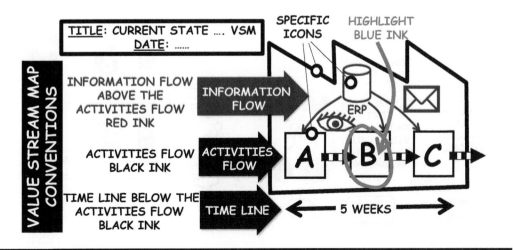

Figure 3.4   VSM Components, Icons and Conventions.

■ Red ink for the information flow
■ Blue ink to make highlights on the map
■ Information flow elements *above* the corresponding activities flow elements
■ Time line elements *below* the activities flow

The icons help graphically display the diverse elements that constitute the map. As we saw in "Can VSM Help?" in Chapter 1, even if VSM is an established practice that uses standard icons for a long time, the particularities of the work performed in a tangled environment call for icons capable of describing confusion, miscommunication, misalignment and conflict. Some of the information flow-specific icons that help to achieve this are described next. As they clearly belong in the information flow, they are captured in red ink:

■ People information, with its different variants: discussion, meeting, chaser (see Figure 3.5–1). The people information and the derived icons reflect the fact that people become the actual bearers of the information and greatly influence what and how information gets shared. Because it is people-based, the information is difficult to record and trace. As we saw in Chapter 2, "Trouble Engaging People?," organizational politics have a big role to play in the way the information is vehiculated: information can be distorted, misdirected, or suppressed in order to manipulate a situation for short-term personal gain, with direct consequences on the activities flow, usually generating defects and delays. Let's consider the situation of a particular manager whose group doesn't deliver to plan and in order to restore the group's image to the organization pressures

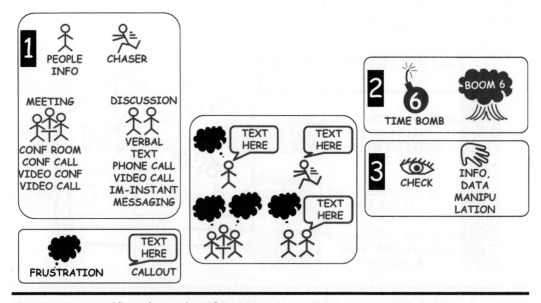

Figure 3.5 Specific Information Flow Icons.

people to deliver regardless of the quality. The short-term gain of delivering to plan, motivated by organizational politics, will be totally upset, though, by the rework required to be done later because of the non-quality. The people information icons help make these situations visible in combination with other icons like callouts, frustration, rework and time bombs. For our example, the manager would be represented with the chaser icon and a callout icon saying, "Just deliver, no matter how!" (see Figure 3.6). The motivation for "just deliver, no matter how!" should be captured and linked with the chaser icon through an information path icon. Figure 3.6 captures three different motivations: (1) the result of "divide and conquer" strategy used by a higher up when subordinates' performances are publicly shared with the intent of making them compete against each other; (2) the result of internal competition when two subordinates (unofficially) compete for a higher-up position in the organization; (3) the result of a company's policies, linking bonuses to targets that are ill-defined.

■ The people information icons can capture triggers to perform work, decision-making, means of working, organizational politics or even conflict. They help identify mainly failure modes, waste of overprocessing and behavioral patterns.

■ Time bomb and boom (see Figure 3.5–2) are used to show the cause and adverse effect as described in "Ready to Record?" In the case of the politically motivated manager, the time bomb icon is positioned next to the chaser icon, and the boom icon is positioned next to where the defects become apparent. They help with identifying mainly failure modes and waste of defects.

Figure 3.6 Combined Use of Icons to Capture Organizational Politics – Alternate Takes.

■ Check and data manipulation (see Figure 3.5–3) are used to illustrate how work is performed and its dependence on people's skills, judgment and attention through verifications, analysis, manual interventions, all required to transform the product. They help with identifying mainly failure modes and waste of overprocessing.

One of the important VSM standard icons is the push arrow. The push arrow is used for linking activities, showing the path for the transformation of the product. It helps highlight how work is pushed from one activity to another in a "throw over the fence" manner. As it is part of the activities flow, it is captured in black ink, and it helps identify indirectly the waste of waiting and inventory.

For a list of suggested icons, please see Appendix B.

3.3.2 How It All Comes Together?

Let's see how it all comes together using the "Modify Drawing" example (can be used by the facilitator to introduce the mapping pattern, the color conventions and the icons used, as suggested in "Everybody on the Same Page?"). To follow the progression, please see Figures 3.7 to 3.14:

Facilitator: Now, let's demonstrate how we will draw the value stream map by using the activity – information – issues mapping pattern. Remember, the color codes we will use are black ink for the activity flow, red ink for the information flow. [Takes a black marker.] So, we start with the activity. [Asks one participant] Just give me a simple example from your daily workload.

Participant: Well, we had this Part X drawing that needed to be modified.

Facilitator: We write the short description of the activity inside a rectangle, with black ink [writing down]. Ok, so the activity is "Modify Drawing Part X." Now, we will capture who performed the activity by drawing the people icon and writing the function and a number specific to the number of persons performing the activity, still using black ink.

Facilitator: [Drawing the people icon and writing] So, you're from engineering, right? You were the only one doing the modification?

Participant: [Smiling] Yes and yes.

Facilitator: [Writing Eng and one next to it] Now, we capture the touch time below the activity, still black ink. How long does it take to modify the drawing if you're not interrupted?

Participant: About 2 hours.

Facilitator: [Writing 2h] How long did it take from when you needed to start modifying until the modification is done? This is the elapsed time, still black ink.

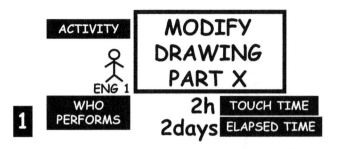

Figure 3.7   Mapping Pattern – Activity Flow.

Participant: Well, it was more than 2 hours … at the time I was working on three different projects, and they were all important.

Facilitator: Ok, in this case, we need to look in the system, see the time stamps of drawing modification … let's say the time stamps from the system show two days … [writing 2 days] (see Figure 3.7).

Participant: Good with me.

Facilitator: Now we start capturing the information [takes the red marker]. What color do we use for the information flow?

Participants: Red ink.

Facilitator: All right! First thing we capture is the trigger, so how did you know you had to modify the drawing?

Participant: Well, I was working on another project, when my boss came along and told me some dimensions changed for Part X … so I was told to modify the drawing as soon as possible.

Facilitator: So, this is a trigger coming from a person. We use the people information icon; then we add a callout [drawing icon and writing "Modify the Drawing!" in the callout]. Then, we show the information path by drawing an arrow from the icon toward the activity, the activity being the recipient (see Figure 3.8).

Facilitator: Now, what's the input for this activity? What do we transform when performing this activity?

Participants: A drawing?

Facilitator: Exactly … this is the drawing icon [draws icon]. We need to add the title and the format name.

Participant: Well, we talk about a ".catpart" file called DWG X revA.

Facilitator: [Writes DWG X rev A above and ".catpart" below] Good. Now, where does this drawing reside?

Participant: In ENOVIA.

Facilitator: [Draws the icon and writes ENOVIA] This is the icon for a database, and we'll name it ENOVIA. We show the information path by drawing an arrow from the database icon to the activity (the activity being the recipient); then we place the drawing icon over the line (see Figure 3.9).

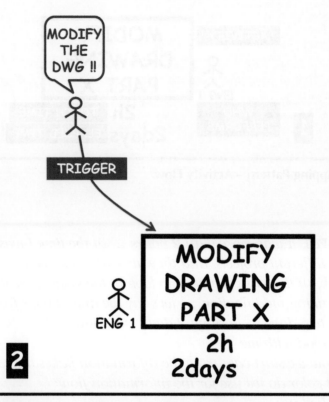

Figure 3.8   Mapping Pattern – Information Flow – Trigger.

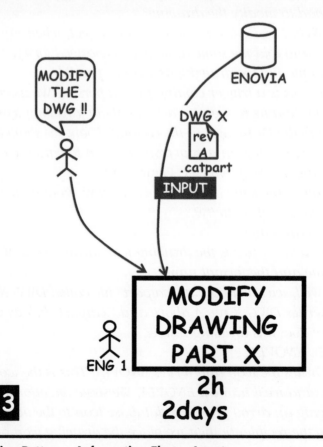

Figure 3.9   Mapping Pattern – Information Flow – Input.

Facilitator: Now, what else do you need to have in order to perform the activity?

Participant: Of course, I needed the new dimensions, which were specified in an email that I received.

Facilitator: The email with the new dimensions is an enabler. [Drawing the email icon] This is the email icon and [writing "new dimensions"] we specify the short title "new dimensions." Two other icons that go with it are [drawing the inbox icon] the inbox icon, where the email arrives and because emails are vehiculated through an email application, we need to capture the database icon [drawing the database icon] specifying the application name – in our case, it's Outlook [writing Outlook below]. As the email was received, we will draw the information path from Outlook [drawing the information path arrow] to the inbox [placing the email icon over the line] and place the email icon over it. Good. Now, what else was required?

Participant: I needed to use the company standard for gaps and overlaps.

Facilitator: So, this standard is another enabler. It's a document, right? [Drawing the document icon] How's it called, what's the format and where does it reside?

Participant: Well, is a ".pdf" file called STD1.0 that is in the eRoom Standards.

Facilitator: [Writing STD1.0 above and .pdf below] Thank you [drawing the database icon and writing eRoom Standards]. Now, we will draw the arrow for the information path – from where to where?

Participants: From the database to the activity.

Facilitator: All right! [drawing the arrow, placing the document icon over the line] (see Figure 3.10). Let's now capture more enablers. Are the drawing and the standard already opened when you want to perform the activity?

Participant: Not really, I have to check and find their location; then I have to open them.

Facilitator: Great, you need to check [drawing the check icon]; this is the icon for checking, and we will place it next to the two databases where you have to look for the documents and of course next to the inbox [placing the icons next to ENOVIA, eRoom Standards, inbox icons].

Facilitator: Now, that you have the drawing, what else do you need in order to modify it? Think in terms of specific software, data manipulation, checks …

Participant: I need all of them … without CATIA, I can't open the drawing; once open I need to check the drawing details; then I need to compare with the standards, do some side analysis, then I manipulate the data in the drawing.

Facilitator: [Drawing the software icon and writing CATIA] So here's the software icon [placing the icon next to the activity]; then we need another check icon [drawing the check icon and placing it next to the

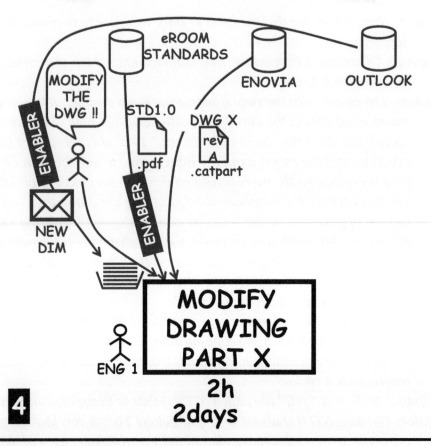

Figure 3.10 Mapping Pattern – Information Flow – Enablers.

*software icon]; then here's the data manipulation icon [drawing the
data manipulation icon and placing it next to the software icon] (see
Figure 3.11). Other enablers?*

Participants: *Coffee!!!*

Facilitator: *[Smiling] Ok, you can go grab some. … Good, so we've completed
the enablers.*

Facilitator: *Next to be captured is the output. What does this activity deliver?
What's the result of the transformation made by the activity?*

Participant: *The new version of the drawing?*

Facilitator: *[Drawing the document icon] I assume it is the same format, and it
goes in the same database [writing ".catpart" below].*

Participant: *Exactly, and the name is DWG X revB.*

Facilitator: *[Writing DWG RevB above] The drawing is saved in ENOVIA, so the
information path goes from the activity to the database icon [draw-
ing an arrow from the activity toward the ENOVIA database, placing
the document icon on the line] (see Figure 3.12). After the output,
we capture the info out. What other information is generated by this
activity? Think in terms of communication, derived data, backup.*

Participant: *Well, I sent an email to my boss, telling that I've finished modifying the drawing.*

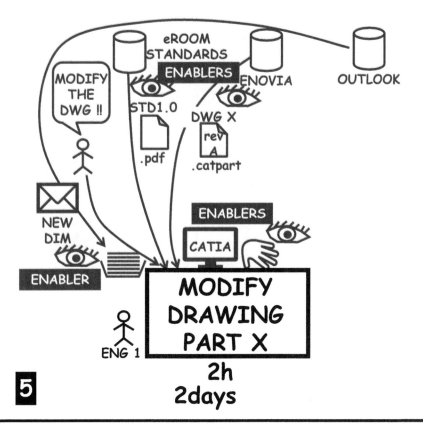

Figure 3.11   Mapping Pattern – Information Flow – More Enablers.

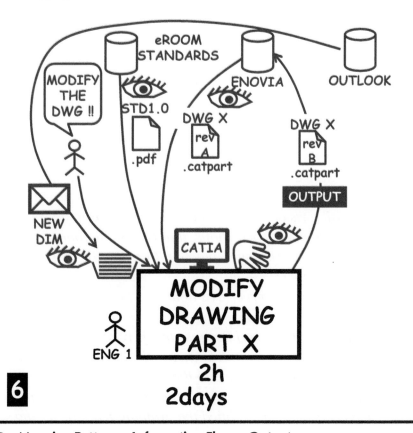

Figure 3.12   Mapping Pattern – Information Flow – Output.

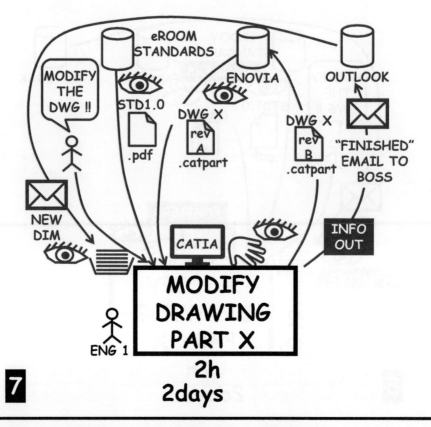

Figure 3.13 Mapping Pattern – Information Flow – Info Out.

Facilitator: Ok [drawing the email icon and writing "finished"], here's the email. As the email is sent, the information path goes from the activity to the Outlook database [drawing an arrow from the activity, pointing to the database, placing the email icon on the line] (see Figure 3.13). Good, now we're ready to capture the issues!

Facilitator: We usually capture the issues as clouds with short text descriptions inside. Depending if the issue is related to the activity itself or with the information, we will use black or red ink [picks the black marker]. Did you face any issues while you were modifying the drawing?

Participant: I got all sorts of error messages, so I needed to figure out what's wrong and to make corrections, that took some time.

Facilitator: [Writing Error Messages, placing it next to the activity] Captured ... other?

Participant: I remember the server was down, so I couldn't get the drawing from ENOVIA.

Facilitator: [Taking a red marker] Because this is related to the information flow, we will use the red ink [drawing the cloud icon and writing Server Down, placing it next to the database]. Something else?

Participant: Ahhh ... I got distracted, so I opened the wrong standard ... a previous version ... I modified the drawing with the wrong specifications ... that was an issue ... luckily, I caught it on time.

Facilitator: [*Drawing the cloud icon, writing Wrong Standard, placing next to the document standard icon*] *Got it! So, when did you realize this?*

Participant: *A day later when I wanted to make sure everything fits nicely together.*

Facilitator: *Then what did you do?*

Participant: *I had to modify the drawing again using the right standard now.*

Facilitator: *Ok, this is the rework icon* [*drawing the rework icon, writing 1*]. *I wrote the number 1, as this is the first rework that we've identified (see Figure 3.14). At this point, we will need a separate sheet of paper where we will record more details about the rework and its impacts. Congratulations team, we've just completed the first mapping pattern!*

Facilitator: *Can someone now read what we've captured on the map?*

Participant: *Let me try … [looking at the map]* (see Figure 3.15); *we modified the drawing Part X from Rev A to Rev B when the boss told us, based on the new dimensions received by email, using the standard STD 1.0, checking files and information and manually modifying the drawing. We had trouble accessing ENOVIA because of the server being down; we had trouble with the CATIA errors, which slowed us down; we had trouble using the wrong standard, which made us rework the*

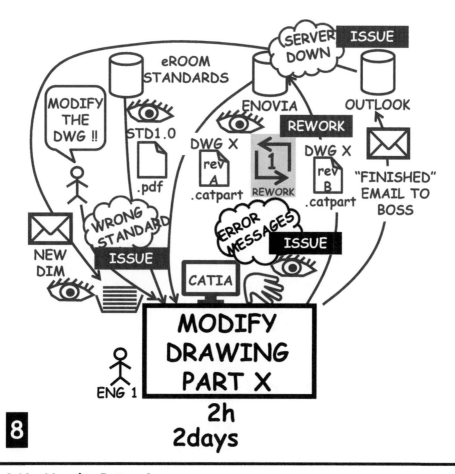

Figure 3.14 Mapping Pattern Issues.

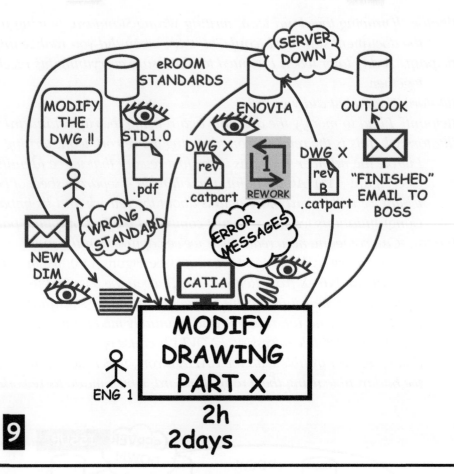

Figure 3.15 Final Result For Mapping Pattern Usage.

*modification. Finally, we sent an email to the boss to say we've finished.
... Oh, and it took us two days to do it when it should have taken 2 h.*
Facilitator: *Excellent! You see, using the mapping pattern makes the reading of
the map easy; it's like telling the story. Of course, there are more icons,
but we'll discover them, as we will map our real case.*

While mapping the current state, we can use the pre-work material to verify
if we've captured all the product transformation stages, if the collected artifacts are captured on the map, answering questions like the following: are
all the stakeholders represented in the map? Did we miss anything? Are there
any areas where we need to explore more?

3.4 Deep Dive or Fly High?

There are different levels of granularity to which a process can be mapped
(see Figure 3.16), each of them having advantages and disadvantages, raising
the question, *What's the right level?* when we value stream map. The
macrolevel has the advantage of covering large cross-functional processes
with few activity boxes and the disadvantage of not allowing us to see the

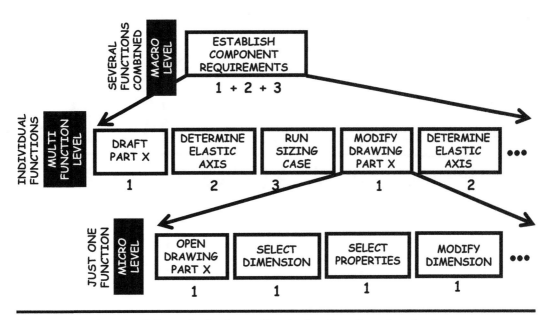

Figure 3.16 Levels of Granularity According to the Functions Involved.

cross-functional exchanges. The microlevel has the advantage of covering in detail the activities and the disadvantage of overwhelming the map in a cross-functional view. Choosing the right level depends on what we want to see, and because in tangled environments the holistic view of the process gets lost, it is recommended to use a macrolevel map first, followed by a multifunction level map. The macrolevel map helps us to take a step back and see the whole, aligning the individual participant's view with the final product and the paying customer. The multifunction level map helps visualize the cross-functional exchanges, clarifying how the individual functions impact each other. It can be done at two levels: a high level for awareness and a detailed level for identification of waste. The macro and the multifunction views are complementary. In a tangled environment, there's a lot of people who don't work directly on the final product that gets delivered but on supporting subprocesses feeding it; therefore, it is appropriate to have a two-stage approach where on a macrolevel map, we position the real case, followed by a multifunction map, where we detail the real case (see Figure 3.17). In most of the exercises I've been involved with, we've settled for a multifunction detailed level map to identify the waste and the failure mechanisms. No matter what approach is taken, it is important to maintain the same level of granularity throughout the whole map. Other considerations for finding the appropriate level of granularity are as follows:

- Project lead time: it's improbable to find the same level of granularity for projects that took years versus projects that took weeks.
- People recognize their daily struggles while transforming the product.
- We can see how the cross functional communication and exchange of information occurs.
- We can see where decisions are being made.

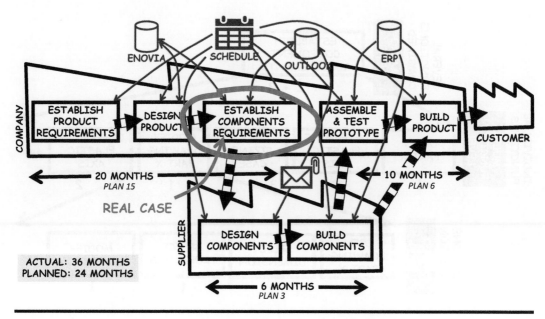

Figure 3.17 Macrolevel Value Stream Map for the New Product.

- We can see where the data is stored and the triggers to perform work.
- There are way too many detailed activities for one function.

Finding the right level is not an exact science; it might take several attempts before nailing it. The use of the aforementioned considerations should help by asking questions like *Do we recognize our daily struggles?* Or, *Do we see how the cross functional exchange of information occurs?*

3.5 Time to Practice

At this point, we will let Ted explain what happened with the late release of mature requirements to the supplier in the new product development program, as introduced in Chapters 1 and 2. Please take some clean sheets of paper, black, red and blue ink pens and follow the narration while drawing the VSM using the mapping pattern. Don't worry if it's not perfect, practice makes it perfect!

Hi, my name is Ted, and I'm a new product development engineering director. Our company recently delivered a new product to the market, and although it was a technical success, we delivered it late and with cost overruns. My group was responsible for the integration of components into the product and had a hard time with a critical component. Our problem statement: mature requirements for the critical component were released five months later than scheduled to the component supplier. During the development work, we've changed our requirements several times, from which about half a dozen were major changes with a big impact on supplier's work. This translated into extra costs because the supplier had to scrap an expensive mold, along with the consequent late delivery of the component.

Before starting to look into the details of how things happened, I would like to introduce you to how our company develops new products, from a 30,000 ft view.

3.5.1 Macrolevel Current State Map

It starts with establishing the product requirements, which includes careful market and business needs analysis, and then continues with designing the product to meet these requirements. Once the overall product design is mature, we start establishing the requirements for the components. Of course, this process is not necessarily sequential or linear, overlaps exist, and a lot of iterations are required. Therefore, determining that the component requirements start much earlier than when the final product design is released. Because of our specific business model, we own the product design, but the diverse component designs are owned by our suppliers, who will build and deliver the parts to our assembly line. So, we send component requirements to our supplier once we make sure critical aspects are not overlooked, especially product safety. We build a prototype using the components delivered by the suppliers; we test it and if the performance meets or exceeds expectations; we start building products that are delivered to customers. The whole process is executed according to a preestablished schedule and managed through governance forums and with the help of project management teams. We mainly use ENOVIA as a repository for the design work, ERP for building prototypes, products and to pay the supplier and Outlook to communicate.

If we talk about the latest development program, regarding the critical component, it took us 20 months from the market and business needs analysis to release mature component requirements to the supplier, 5 months later than planned. It took the supplier six months to design and build the component and ten months for us to build and test the prototype and then to actually build and deliver the product. This all added up to 36 months, 12 months later than the planned 24-month schedule. Our objective going into the VSM exercise was to cut the component release time for mature requirements in half.

Let's look at the suggested map (see Figure 3.17). The activities flow comprises big chunks of work, showing through push arrows how the product is transformed from requirements to finished product in the hands of the customer. You notice the three big entities involved – namely, the company, the supplier and the customer. Even though Ted mentioned some parallelism between designing the product and establishing component requirements, the activities were presented in series for simplicity reasons, as the main objective of the macrolevel is to position the process under scrutiny in the big picture, to build a common understanding on who the customer is, what's the finished product and how we contribute to it. As you can see, the information flow is sketchy, showing just the big pieces required for the transformation: schedule as a trigger, ENOVIA and ERP as repositories, Outlook and email with attachment for communication. This is ok, as we are not using the macrolevel to identify waste but for positioning. The positioning is done in blue ink. The time line was placed under the respective activities, showing the planned and the actual durations. Let's hear Ted:

> *Now I would like to introduce you to how we establish requirements for the component from a 5,000 ft generic view.*

3.5.2 *High-Level Current State Map*

We're part of the integration "INTG" engineering function, responsible for the integration of components into the product, and we're the middleman between several other specialized engineering functions, the program organization and the supplier. What we're really taking care of is the impact the design of the components has on the overall product performance, with a focus on safe product operation. In order to achieve a safe design, specific analysis on critical components is performed by the Failsafe "FSAF" specialized engineering function under several conditions called the "fully operative case," which typically serves to size the components. The analysis results clearly show if the product will operate safely or not. In case the result is "fail," we need to decide what adjustments to the component's characteristics are required in order to make the product safe. The adjustments are decided during meetings where the analysis results are presented. The analysis itself is performed using an "FSAF" specific model requiring inputs from the Mechanical "MECH," Structural "STRU" and Thermoelectrical "THEL" specialized engineering functions. Several iterations taking a lot of time are required in order to achieve the component's characteristics granting safe product operation. Once we have a "pass," a second analysis is performed by the same "FSAF" group, with the same model requiring inputs from "MECH," "STRU" and "THEL," this time considering the "end of life case." This might take some time too because of the inherent iterations. … Finally, after the "pass" on the second analysis, we send the modifications to the Design "DSGN" engineering function, which updates the drawings; then we contact the Configuration Management "CMGT" function, which checks and updates the product configuration and derives the requirements from the drawing in an official document called a "memo," which is sent to the supplier as an email attachment. The coordination between the different tasks is done through email using Outlook. Each engineering function is using its own model to provide inputs or to perform analysis. We use eRoom to store the analysis results, minutes of meetings, presentations and memos, and we use ENOVIA and CATIA for the drawings. All stakeholders work to meet scheduled dates.

In our specific case, the component requirements development and the product design were planned to run in parallel for a duration of seven months, with the parallelism ending when the product design was mature, with an additional three months allowing for mature component requirements, for a total 10-month plan. The 12 weeks (3 months) were divided into two 6-week cycles, each cycle comprising 5 weeks of iterations and 1 week for updating the drawing and deriving the requirements. This meant three releases for the component requirements: the draft, corresponding to when the product design is mature; the intermediary, corresponding to 6 weeks after; and the final, corresponding to the 12 weeks after (see Figure 3.18). The reality was far from this though … due to finding errors late in the process, we delivered valid requirements to the supplier in 15 months, when the plan was 10 months. They even had to scrap an expensive mold due to our errors.

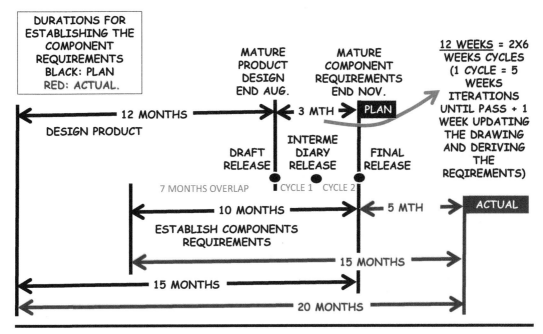

Figure 3.18   Durations for Establishing the Component Requirements.

Let's look at the suggested map for the current state (see Figure 3.19). The first thing to notice is the entities corresponding to the main players: seven engineering functions and the supplier. The activities flow includes the main activity performed by each of them, as this is a high-level multifunction map linked with push arrows depicting the transformation path from providing inputs to requirements received by the supplier. Please note the split of paths at the decision point: continue to "Modify Drawing" if it's a "pass"

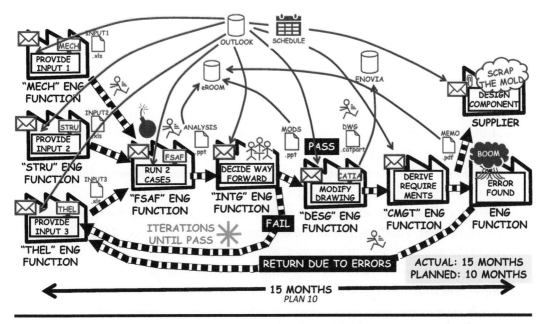

Figure 3.19   High-Level Current State VSM for the Critical Component Requirements to Supplier.

and return to "Provide Inputs" if it's a "fail." The blue star next to the return path identifies the loop for iterations. Ted mentioned performing the fully operative case and the end-of-life case, but at this high level, the activities are covered by a generic one called "Run 2 Cases." The iteration loops include both the decision going forward and the situation when the "fully operative case" is a "pass," and we decide to start the "end of life case." Don't forget, the intent behind the multifunction high-level map is to give a general view of how the required players interact. Capturing in a serial way showing the two cases would have been a valid way too. The only disadvantage to this is the map becomes bigger. There's no touch time or elapsed time, with the time line being represented by the total duration, which includes all the returns in the process due to finding errors.

Looking at the information flow, please note the main transformation stages of this process's product, the requirements: inputs – analysis results – modifications – drawing – requirements, reflected in several *.xls, .ppt, .catpart, .pdf* documents constituting the outputs of the respective activities. At this level, it's not necessary to capture all the mapping pattern elements, so you'll notice that the inputs are not captured. The triggers to perform work are represented by the email icons coming from Outlook, and the enablers are captured by the computer model icons and the meeting icon. The schedule icon shows the focal point for everybody. The time bomb and the boom icons represent where the errors were generated and when they surfaced, with the addition of the cloud icon showing the scrapping of the mold. The chaser icon illustrates the main trigger to perform work.

Ted continues: *So, here's the detailed story. Please note this is a simplified but relevant version, as going too deep into the complicated technical details could easily blur the essence:*

> *This product being by far our most ambitious in terms of performance, we made sure we understood well its requirements, which were far more demanding than our previous products. The initial sizing of the product gave us the starting point for components' characteristics, which needed to be designed to withstand severe, never encountered before conditions. A first set of analysis was done by "FSAF" to assess how safe the component was. Because we were in preliminary stages, component data was not mature, so we took the approach of using mature component data from an existing product, which was the closest in terms of performance. We basically took the existing component and plugged it into the new product; then "FSAF" performed the analysis – it was a "pass." Then we used the new component immature data, and "FSAF" did the analysis again – it was a "pass." As both analysis results were positive, we got the warm and fuzzy feeling we were on the right path. After a couple of weeks, a new internal report from "MECH" came out. As the product design evolved, substantial changes in the component's stiffness were made. This was communicated through email to all the concerned parties.*

3.5.3 Detailed-Level Current State Map

So, we stared officially on January 23, as per the schedule: "MECH" determined the elastic axis and the stiffness for the component using the model "MECH" and sent them to "FSAF" for the analysis in an .xls file hosted in the "MECH" eRoom. At the same time, based on the change, "STRU" determined the mass distribution of the component using the model "STRU" then sent it to "FSAF" in an .xls file, hosted in the "STRU" eRoom, and "THEL" determined the thermoelectrics of the component using the model "THEL" and then sent it to "FSAF" in an .xls file hosted in the "THEL" eRoom. They all used the same .catpart component drawing from ENOVIA and the minutes of meetings detailing the modifications to do their work, and they all attached the .xls files in their Outlook email messages to "FSAF." "FSAF" performed the analysis using their "FSAF" model and captured the output in their "FSAF" eRoom as a ".f06" file. It was a "fail." They immediately contacted us "INTG" and we called a meeting to look at the possible failure mechanisms and find a way forward, inviting "MECH," "STRU" and "THEL" too. What is important to know is that these people are not dedicated exclusively to this particular project; they have other projects to take care of. Because of that, everybody had different priorities, so we needed to do some chasing to get them together. During the meeting, "FSAF" presented a .ppt hosted in the "FSAF" eRoom detailing the data from the analysis; then the decision was made to increase the component's thickness by an amount deemed enough to counter the exposed failure mechanism. We "INTG" transferred the .ppt in our "INTG" eRoom, along with the minutes of the meeting containing the decision and the subsequent actions; then we emailed them to the participants. This meant another round of "MECH," "STRU" and "THEL" runs of their respective models with the modified data and another round of .xls files that were sent to "FSAF." It was a "fail." Another meeting, still busy schedules, chases … When the meeting finally happened, the decision was to keep the new thickness but to change the material orientation. We "INTG" transferred the .ppt in our "INTG" eRoom, along with the minutes of the meeting containing the decision and the subsequent actions; then we emailed them to the participants … another round of "MECH," "STRU" and "THEL" runs of their respective models with the modified data and another round of .xls files sent to "FSAF." "Fail" again. Another meeting, still busy schedules, chases, decision to keep the modifications but to move the location of the component's attachments. We "INTG" transferred the .ppt in our "INTG" eRoom, along with the minutes of the meeting containing the decision and the subsequent actions, which then were emailed to the participants … another round of "MECH," "STRU" and "THEL" runs of their respective models with the modified data and another round of .xls files sent to "FSAF." Still a "fail." After another couple of chases and meetings, changing again thicknesses, we finally got the "pass" in an email from FSAF. We "INTG" immediately contacted "DSGN," which then updated the component's geometry in the CATIA .catpart drawing residing in ENOVIA. At the same time, we were ourselves being chased by the project people to deliver the first draft of requirements to the supplier. They were saying, "Our VP talked with the supplier VP, and they agreed to send some data, as their manpower was sitting idle." We knew that we still needed to run the "end of life case," but we deemed it ok to have a draft that didn't include it, so we contacted "CMGT," which derived the requirements from the updated drawing and sent the memo with the requirements in a .pdf document, attached to an email to the supplier, where we "INTG" were cc'd. We archived the email and the .pdf in our "INTG" eRoom; then we had to take care of another priority. It was March 13.

CHECKPOINT: Did you draw something similar (see Figure 3.26)? One can admit, throwing out a picture like this and trying to read it becomes overwhelming. Do not forget though that we're building the map with the mapping pattern, one activity at a time. What you see here is the final result, starting with the inputs and ending with the first release of requirements. Please note how the convention of keeping the information flow above the activities flow is applied. Looking just at the activities and the push arrows, one can notice a similar pattern with the previous map – we have the return push arrow and the iterations icon for the "fail" and another push arrow for the "pass." This time though, the two cases run by FSAF are not mixed together generically, we can clearly see the "run fully operative case" as a distinctive activity. The time line captures the period from January 23 when the MECH, STRU and THEL activities started to run in parallel, to March 13, corresponding to the requirements being sent to the supplier. What you can acknowledge is the richness of the information flow, as inputs, outputs, triggers, info out and enablers are captured for each activity.

But let's start from the beginning and go step-by-step, using the mapping pattern.

The MECH engineering function performs in parallel two main activities (see Figure 3.20): "determine and send elastic axis" and "determine and send component stiffness." Because they are using the same inputs and enablers, the information flow is placed on top of the first activity, with the other activity being placed just underneath. The people icon with the MECH name under it indicates who physically performs the activities; no number next to it means that the same person performs both of them. Now, let's look at the information flow. We can see the triggers, represented by the chaser icon and by the email icon, coming from the Outlook icon; note that the email contains the minutes of the meeting detailing the modifications, and for this reason, it is an input too. The other input is the ".catpart" drawing icon coming from the ENOVIA icon. The enablers are captured with the check icon, data manipulation icon and the MECH software icon. The output is the ".xls" file icon with the elastic axis and with the stiffness going in the MECH eRoom icon. The info out is the email with the attachment icon sent to FSAF through the Outlook icon. The email itself is used as a trigger, and the attachment is used as an input by the FSAF activity not pictured yet; there's just the push arrow pointing toward it. The time line start date is captured at the bottom.

Another activity happening in parallel is performed by STRU (see Figure 3.21) and called "determine and send component mass distribution." The same convention is applied: information flow above the activity flow.

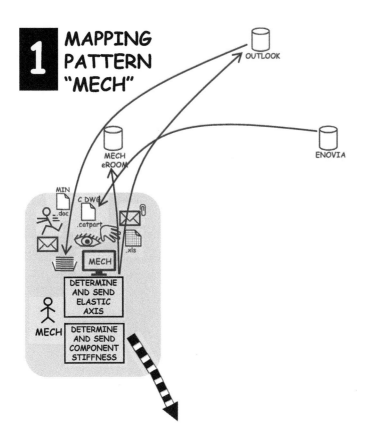

Figure 3.20   Mapping Pattern "MECH."

The people icon with STRU below indicates there's a single person physically performing the activity. The information flow has the same inputs and triggers as the MECH activities: the email with the minutes of the meeting containing the modifications and the chaser. The enablers are similar, except for the STRU model used. The output is similar, except that the ".xls" file icon contains the mass distribution and is going in the STRU eRoom icon. The info out is similar to the outgoing email containing the file with the mass

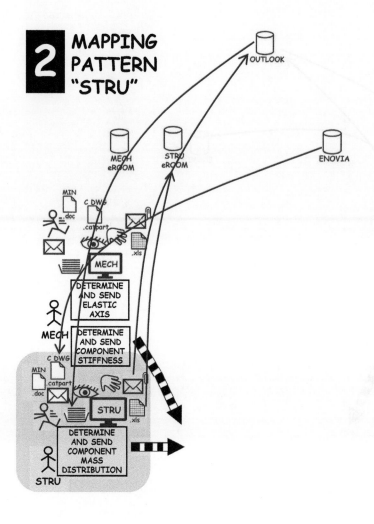

Figure 3.21 Mapping Pattern "STRU."

distribution. The email itself is used as a trigger, and the attachment is used as an input by the FSAF activity not pictured yet; there's just the push arrow pointing toward it. The time line shows the same starting date: January 23.

"Determine and send thermoelectrics," performed by THEL (see Figure 3.22) starts at the same time as the other activities presented earlier. As you can see, the information flow looks similar to the already captured

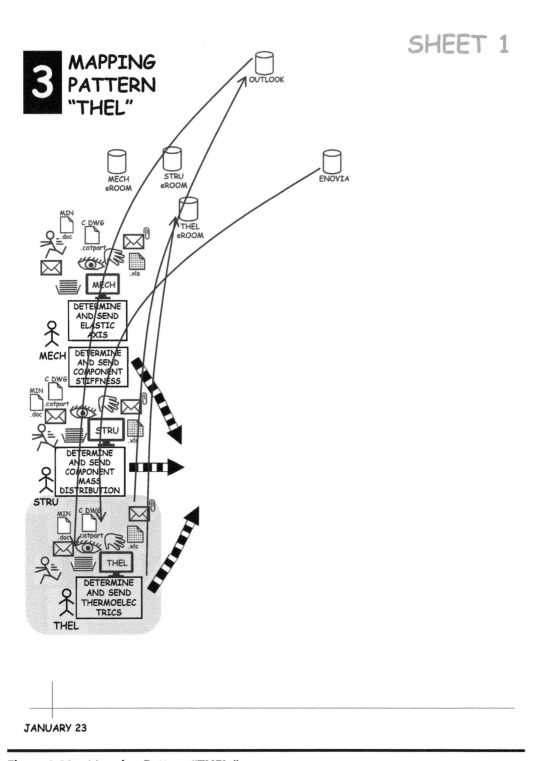

Figure 3.22   Mapping Pattern "THEL."

ones, except for the THEL model used, and the ".xls" file icon containing the thermoelectrics, going in the THEL eRoom icon.

What comes next? With all the inputs available, FSAF runs the "fully operative case" (see Figure 3.23) by one person, as represented by the people icon. There's always the possibility to link at a later stage the previous

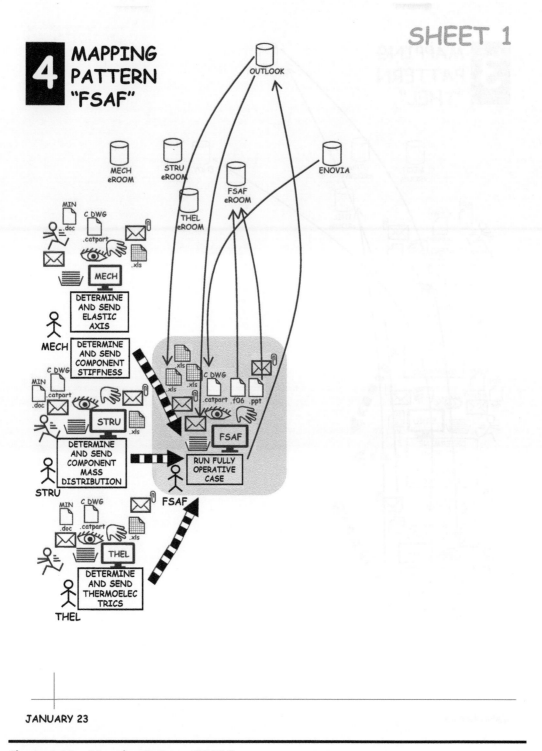

Figure 3.23   Mapping Pattern "FSAF."

activities with the current one by the push arrows. In this example, we captured the push arrows after each activity, but it's perfectly ok to draw them later. Looking at the information flow, we can see the inputs: three ".xls" files icons coming as attachments from the Outlook icon, along with the ".catpart" drawing coming from ENOVIA icon. We can see the enablers: the FSAF software icon, the check icon, the data manipulation icon. The

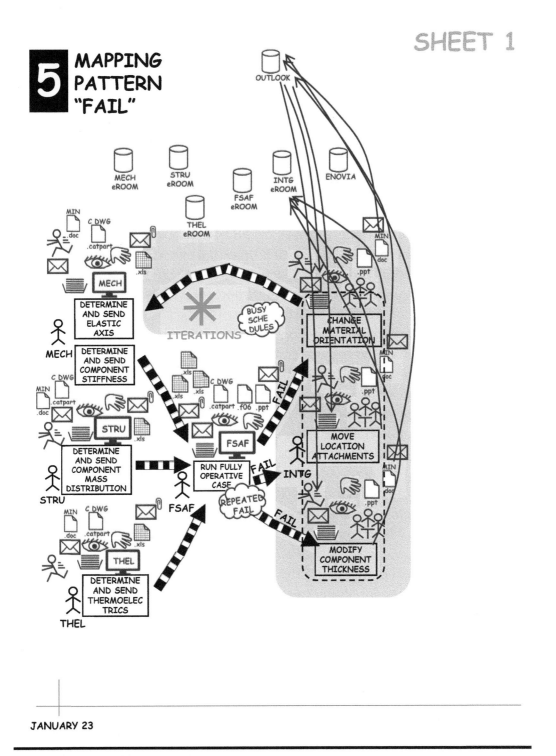

Figure 3.24   Mapping Pattern "FAIL."

outputs are the ".f06" file icon and the ".ppt" file icon, both going in the FSAF eRoom icon. The info out is the ".ppt" file sent as an attachment to INTG. The triggers to perform work are multiple: the three attachments coming from MECH, STRU, THEL and another email coming from INTG.

What happens when the analysis result is a "fail"? (see Figure 3.24). The paths are represented by the three push arrows with "fail" written over them.

We could have represented the activities in a series: first, "modify thickness" then return to another iteration; second, "change material orientation" and the return to another iteration; third, "move location attachments" and the return to another iteration. Doing it that way would have been perfectly good, with the disadvantage of taking a lot of space going to the right. Instead, the three activities are represented in parallel, even though they take place sequentially, with a dotted line box circling them, meaning that just one activity from the three could happen at a time. A single INTG people icon shows that any of the three activities is performed by the same person. From the dotted line box, there's the return push arrow with the iteration icon next to it, meaning that any of the activities in the dotted box follow this return path. Let's follow the possible paths: first time "fail" we can choose to change the material orientation and then go back where the three functions provide the corresponding inputs, feeding another run of the fully operative case, with a second "fail." Now, we choose to move the location of the attachments and go back where the three functions provide the corresponding inputs, feeding another run of the fully operative case, with a third "fail." This time, we choose to modify the thickness and go back where the three functions provide the corresponding inputs, feeding another run of the fully operative case; we can do any of these loops multiple times until we get a "pass." If we look at the information flow for each activity, they are similar: the trigger is represented by the chaser icon and by the email invitation icon coming from the Outlook icon. The input is the ".ppt" file icon representing the analysis results and sent as an attachment by FSAF to INTG that goes in the INTG eRoom. The enablers are the meeting icon, the check icon and the data manipulation icon. The output is the ".doc" file icon containing the minutes of the meeting and the actions that go to the INTG eRoom. The info out is the email icon that has the minutes of the meeting and the actions copied inside from the ".doc" document, going to the Outlook icon. This email becomes an input for MECH, STRU and THEL to make the appropriate modifications in their models and to perform their calculations that will become another set of inputs to FSAF. Two issues are captured at this stage: "busy schedules," which covers the difficulty of gathering all the required players at the same table, and "repeated fail," showing that there were more fails than expected.

Once the result is a "pass" (see Figure 3.25) the coordination activity of "confirm component passes" is performed by INTG, as the people icon shows. The push arrow coming from the "run fully operative case" has written "pass" next to it. As you notice, new triggers appear in the information flow. Remember what Ted was saying? *At the same time, we were ourselves being chased by the project people to deliver the first draft of requirements to the supplier. They were saying, "Our VP talked with the supplier VP, and they agreed to send some data, as their manpower was sitting idle."* Please note how this was captured: next to the supplier icon, there's the meeting icon with "senior management" written below it and with the callout icon "our people are idle."

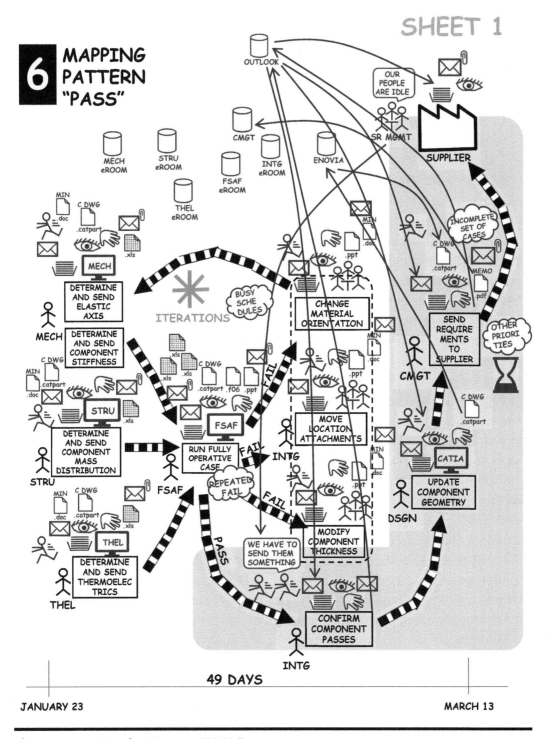

Figure 3.25 Mapping Pattern "PASS."

This represents the VP discussion that triggered the project people to chase the INTG people, as represented by the chase the chaser icon with the callout icon "we have to send them something." The other trigger is represented by the email icon coming from the Outlook icon, representing the email sent by FSAF to confirm the "pass." The enablers are the check icon and the data manipulation icon. The info out is the email icon going to the Outlook icon, sent by INTG to DSGN and CMGT to coordinate the release and containing the modifications to the component. The next activity, "update component geometry" with the DSGN people icon next to it is linked to the previous one by the push arrow. The triggers are represented by the email icon coming from the Outlook icon sent by INTG in the previous activity and by the chaser icon. The enablers are represented by the check icon, data manipulation icon and the CATIA software icon. The output is represented by the ".catpart" drawing going to ENOVIA icon. The last activity is "send requirements to supplier," which is linked to the previous one with the push arrow and has the people icon next to it indicating that it's performed by CMGT. The triggers are represented by the email icon coming from the Outlook icon sent by INTG in the previous activity and by the chaser icon. The enablers are represented by the check icon, data manipulation icon and by the ".catpart" modified drawing coming from ENOVIA. The output is the configuration modification in the CMGT tool and the ".pdf" memo file containing the requirements. The info out is the email with attachment icon going to the Outlook icon that is sent to the supplier, representing the release of the requirements. The issue of sending requirements without completing the "end of life case" is captured next to this activity. Above the supplier icon, you can see the email with attachment icon and the check icon, representing the arrival of the requirements. The picture is complete with the waiting icon and the cloud icon of "working on other priorities," meaning that nothing was done until later to continue working on requirements. Please note the bottom to top chain of activities, leading to the supplier – going horizontally would have been perfectly ok, with the disadvantage of taking more space as we go to the right. This vertical display is justified by the fact that the activities are separated by small time intervals (this is relative to the total lead time). The March 13 time stamp is set in line with sending the requirements and defines the time line from the start of the process until the first release of requirements, corresponding to 49 calendar days. This all brings us to the composed image (see Figure 3.26) shown at the beginning.

Please apply the notions mentioned previously while Ted continues the detailed story:

> *While keeping an eye on the schedule, we started to chase "MECH," "STRU" and "THEL" to provide their inputs to "FSAF" to proceed with the "end of life case" analysis. April 4, the machine started to spin again: "MECH" determined the elastic axis and the stiffness for the component using the model "MECH" and sent them to "FSAF" for the analysis in an .xls file hosted in the "MECH" eRoom. At the same time, "STRU" determined the mass distribution of the component using the model "STRU" and then sent it to "FSAF" in an .xls file hosted in the "STRU" eRoom, and "THEL" determined the thermoelectrics of the component using the model "THEL" and then sent it to "FSAF," in an*

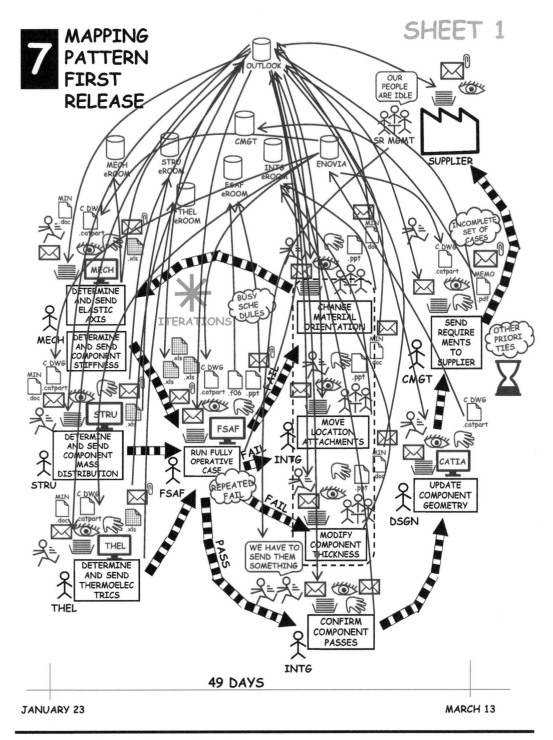

Figure 3.26 Mapping Pattern First Release.

.xls file hosted in the "THEL" eRoom. They all used the updated .catpart component drawing from ENOVIA and the minutes of the meeting detailing the modifications to do their work, and they all attached the .xls files in their Outlook email messages to "FSAF." "FSAF" performed the analysis using their "FSAF" model and captured the output in their

"FSAF" eRoom as a .f06 file. It was a "fail." Another round of meetings happened, peppered with chases between busy schedules, failures and .ppt presentations, where the decisions were made to modify the attachment stiffness and to locally modify the component thickness, in zone 23. Of course, the usual "go back and do the analysis" for "MECH," "STRU" and "THEL" happened, along with their .xls email attachments sent to "FSAF," our "INTG" eRoom being populated with the .ppt's and with the minutes of meetings emailed to the participants ... that is, until we finally got a "pass." We "INTG" then contacted "DSGN," who updated the components' and attachment's characteristics in the .catpart drawing residing in ENOVIA, and then we contacted "CMGT," who derived the requirements from the updated drawing and sent the requirements in a .pdf format attached to an email to the supplier. The memo went out May 1, and we started working on other priorities, pertinently knowing that there are other changes coming. We felt comfortable though because we knew that the product design wouldn't be mature before the end of August, and the component's final requirements were required for November: the date when the supplier needed to start machining the mold according to the schedule.

About one week later, we got a meeting invite from the "FSAF" specialist. It was about a finding they made: the elastic axis in their model "FSAF" was incorrectly represented because of the meshing differences with the "MECH" model. They'd found a solution and worked out the differences, but the consequence was they needed to restart the analysis from the beginning. On May 7th, we were back to square one. Imagine the frustration! [end of story for sheet 1].

CHECKPOINT: This is how the second release map could look (see Figure 3.27). You can see the similarities of the activities flow with what was mapped in the first release: the activities performed by MECH, STRU, THEL linked with the "run end of life case" performed by FSAF, the two "fail" paths, with the "modify thickness zone 23" and "modify attachment stiffness" happening one at a time in the dotted line box and the return push arrow for the iterations; the "pass" path going from INTG to DSGN, CMGT and, finally, to the supplier. What's different is the starting and the ending activities. The starting activity is the "push for next case" (most to the left) performed by INTG and linked to the activities performed by MECH, STRU and THEL by the three push arrows. The activities ending this part of the story are "correct meshing mismatch" performed by FSAF and "determine the way forward" performed by INTG. As you notice, there's no push arrow between "correct meshing mismatch" and the previous activities, as they are not linked by inputs and outputs. The same applies to the "push for the next case" activity. In the information flow attached to it, we can see the trigger represented by the people info icon next to the schedule and check icon. What this

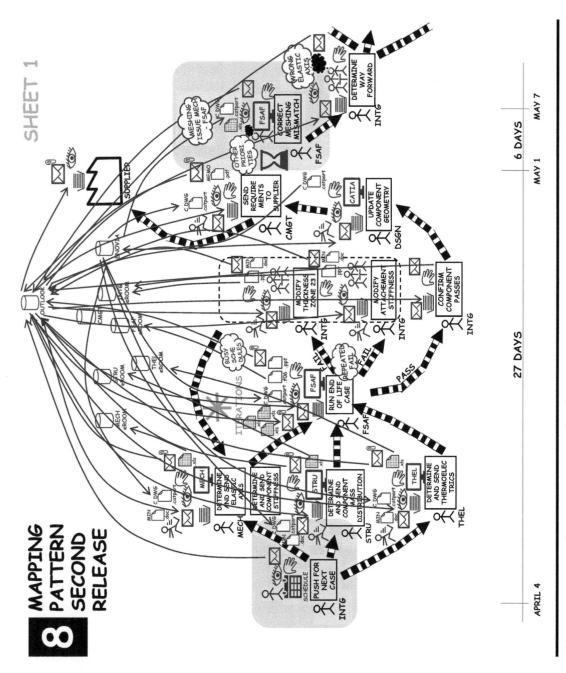

Figure 3.27 Mapping Pattern Second Release.

means is the activity was performed when someone checked the schedule and deemed it necessary to reengage with the others to run the necessary second case. The enabler is the data manipulation icon; the info out is the email icon going to the Outlook icon. The "correct meshing mismatch" activity has a similar trigger: the people info icon with a dark cloud next to it. This represents the frustrating moment when the FSAF person realized there's a meshing issue, triggering the model correction. The inputs are the ".xls" file icon containing the elastic axis, the FSAF model icon and the ".catpart" drawing icon. The enablers are the checking and data manipulation icons. The output is the corrected model and the info out is the email icon going to the Outlook icon, notifying INTG about the situation. The issue captured in the cloud icon is the "meshing issue MECH – FSAF." The trigger for the last activity is the email icon coming from the Outlook icon, representing the meeting invite. The enabler is the meeting icon with the dark cloud expressing people's frustration, the check icon and the data manipulation icon. The info out is the email icon going to the Outlook icon, notifying the participants about the situation and the way forward. The issue captured in the cloud icon is "wrong elastic axis," meaning that because of the meshing issue, the elastic axis was wrongly represented in the FSAF model (for the entire Sheet 1 please see Appendix C1).

Please continue mapping the narration. Ted continues:

> *"FSAF" took all the .xls files provided by "MECH," "STRU" and "THEL" and ran the "fully operative case" with the corrected model. It was a "fail." Another round of iterations started, with all the related activities: chases, meetings, running the specific models, decisions, emailing minutes of meetings … until the "pass." There was thickness, material orientation modifications, modifications to the location of the attachments. This resulted in a new component drawing and a new set of requirements for the supplier, as the same motivation to keep the supplier's people busy was pressuring us to deliver. The memo went out June 19, and we had to shift our attention to other priorities.*
>
> *Then … about one week later, we got another meeting invitation from "FSAF." They were accompanied by "THEL" … this time around it was the thermoelectric distribution in the "FSAF" model being wrongly represented due to a meshing error in the "THEL" model. "THEL" corrected and confirmed the right meshing in their model, but this meant we were back to square one again … it was June 27. Frustration started building again, as November didn't look very far now, while we were all wondering if there aren't any other bad surprises lurking out there.*

CHECKPOINT: please compare (see Figure 3.28) with the story and identify main activities flow points and the corresponding main information flow points, then compare with what you've captured. Ask yourself: are the activities

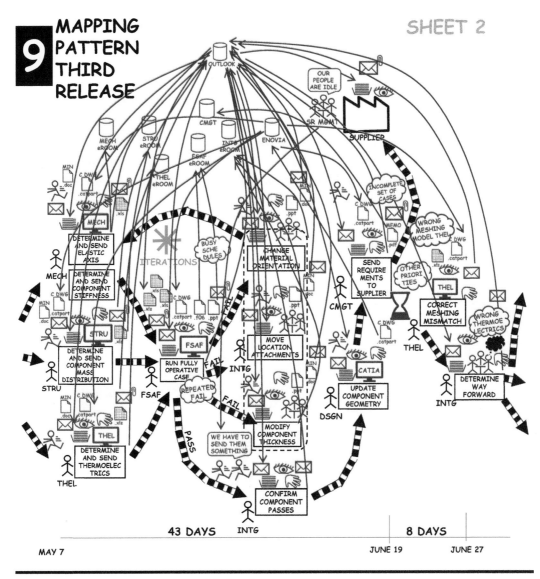

Figure 3.28 Mapping Pattern Third Release.

well connected through the push arrows? Do they follow the storyline? Are the triggers, inputs, enablers, outputs and info out represented for each activity?

Please continue mapping the narration. Ted continues:

So, "FSAF" took the .xls files provided by "MECH" and "STRU," updated according to the latest product design and ran the "fully operative case" with the corrected input from "THEL." "Fail." Another round of iterations started in the worst period of the year, the summer vacation: chases, meetings, running the specific models, decisions, emailing minutes of meetings … until we had the "pass." The confirmation email brought to the attention of senior management the various issues we had so far. There was component thickness, material orientation and attachment location modifications. All of these resulted into a new component drawing being released and a new set of requirements sent to the supplier, without the "end of life case" done, as the schedule pressure became more stringent. The supplier requirements memo was released on August 22. So, the senior leadership team decided, because of the potential slippage, to bring this matter into the program risk governance meeting, managed by the Program organization, held on a weekly basis and attended by senior management. This is where I got to work more closely with Frank and with the "MECH," "STRU," "THEL" and "FSAF" management. For each risk management meeting we needed to present a ".ppt" file with updates, that we needed to save in the PROG eRoom and our own eRoom. On August 26 we started another cycle of iterations. [end of story for Sheet 2]

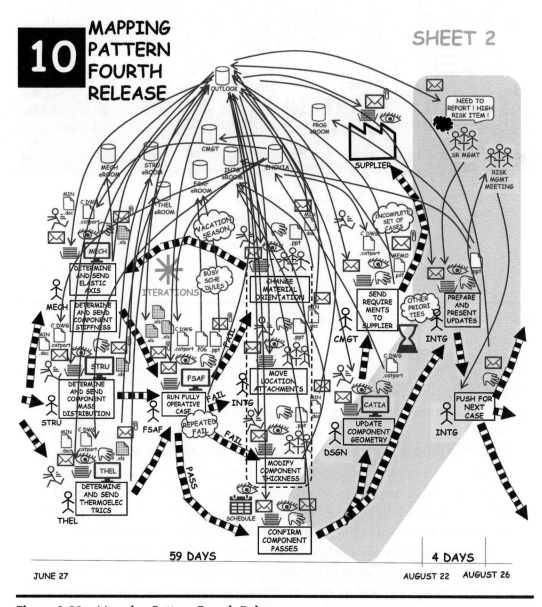

Figure 3.29   Mapping Pattern Fourth Release.

CHECKPOINT: Please compare (see Figure 3.29) with the story and identify main activities flow points and the corresponding main information flow points, and then compare with what you've captured. Please make sure you've captured the cloud icon "vacation season" next to the iteration icon, the frustrated senior leadership meeting icon as a trigger to "prepare and present updates" reporting activity, the risk management meeting icon and the PROG eRoom icon. As you will notice, there's a push arrow between "confirm component passes" and "prepare and present updates," showing they are linked by the confirmation email sent by INTG and used by senior management to trigger the reporting. The output of "prepare and present updates" is the ".ppt" file icon that goes to the two eRoom icons: PROG and INTG and in the risk management meeting icon. Then this meeting becomes the trigger to perform the "push for next case" activity (for the entire Sheet 2 please see Appendix C2).

Please continue mapping the narration. Ted continues:

> *While working on the "end of life case," we had several "fails," which forced us to modify the component's thickness in zone 45 and to modify the attachment stiffness. At the same time, we were preparing ".ppt" presentations, saved in the PROG eRoom and INTGR eRoom, for the risk management governance meetings, where we were required to present on a weekly basis. After we finally got to "pass" we lost about two days because we ran out of CATIA licenses. ... The supplier requirements memo went out on September 25. Everybody was relieved as we were finally in good shape for the November deadline ... our KPI (Key Performance Indicator) turned green.*

CHECKPOINT: The new situation introduced in this part of the story is the governance forums, in the form of risk management meetings. So, how did you capture them? Here's a suggested view (see Figure 3.30). Some considerations behind the choices: they are happening at fixed intervals; preparation is time-consuming; they are more status oriented (touching the product but not transforming it). For these reasons, they were captured according to the time line: in the 30 days covered, there were 5 risk management meetings, an icon for each. Because the work of preparing and presenting happened intertwined with the work on iterations, the activity "prepare and present updates" was included in the dotted line square just once, even if it happened five times. As a reminder, the dotted line square means that just one activity from the three could happen at a time. It's the information flow that connects the activity icon with the change management meetings icons – see the information path arrows. We can see that the trigger for the activity comes from the Outlook icon, as an email icon, representing the meeting invitation. The enablers are the check icon and the data manipulation icon, with the output and the info out being the ".ppt" file icon, that is presented in the meeting

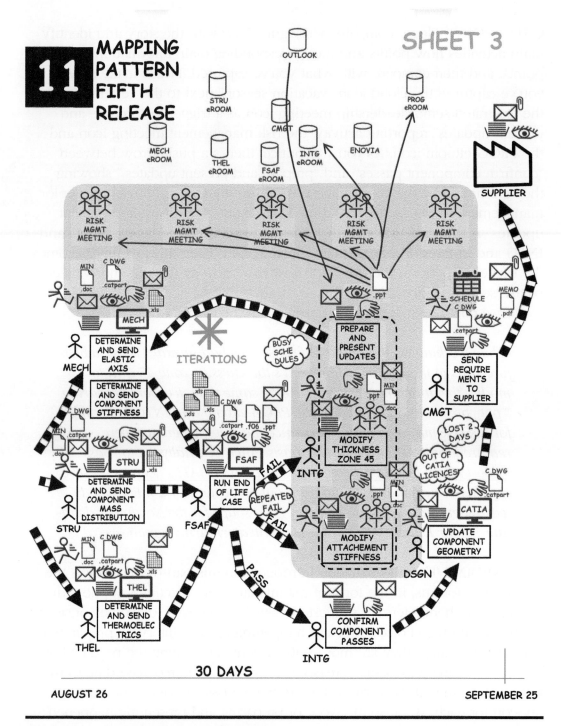

Figure 3.30   Mapping Pattern Fifth Release.

(information path to the meeting icon) and stored in the INTG eRoom and PROG eRoom (see information path to both eRoom icons).

Please continue mapping the narration. Ted continues:

> *Then the unexpected happened: during the scheduled design peer review with engineering specialists from another new development*

program, it became apparent that we were working with the wrong sizing case. Because of the severe conditions, the component was exposed to (never encountered by our other products), the sizing case was not the "fully operative case," but the "attachment case." The implication was we needed to run now three cases instead of two. Back to square one. It was October 11 when we started the new iteration cycle.

In order to run the "attachment case," the "FSAF" model needed to be modified, and "MECH" needed to run the "ATCH" model in order to provide attachment stiffness input to "FSAF." The "ATCH" model was already used in another new development program, so they felt comfortable using it. The other required inputs were provided using the latest model corrections and the latest product data: "MECH" determined the elastic axis and the stiffness of the component; "STRU" determined the mass distribution of the component; "THEL" determined the thermoelectrics of the component. They all used the same .catpart component drawing from ENOVIA and the minutes of the meeting detailing the modifications to do their work, and they all attached the .xls files in their Outlook email messages to "FSAF." The "fail" triggered another series of chases and meetings, this time happening faster because of the scrutiny in the governance forum and the pressure to deliver on time. We played again with component thickness, attachment location and attachment stiffness until we got the "pass." The supplier got the requirements memo on November 12, so we claimed the on-time release of the mature requirements. It was a political move to show we delivered on time, motivated by the bonus scheme, even if the other two required cases were not run yet.

Please note: the supplier already started working on the component design in March, modifying it as we went along. As the component design changed, the mold design changed too. This is a complicated mold with sophisticated, oversized geometry, from a special alloy that needed to withstand severe conditions and requiring multiple special tools and jigs in order to be fabricated. The mold design freeze was imposed by the long fabrication lead time for the mold, an item on the project critical path. So, the supplier launched the mold in fabrication, with some allowance for fine-tuning (end of story for Sheet 3).

CHECKPOINT: So, how did you capture the narration? There are several points to consider (see Figure 3.31, letters a to d):

a) The "review design" activity. As you notice, this activity is performed by a group of people, represented by the black ink three people icons. For the information flow, the trigger is the schedule icon, the inputs are the

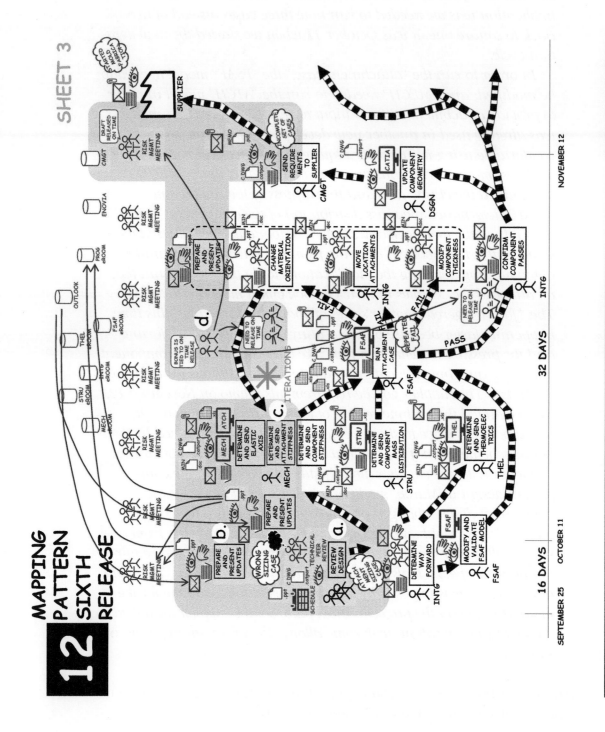

Figure 3.31   Mapping Pattern Sixth Release.

".ppt" file icon and the ".catpart" icon. The enabler is the check icon and the "technical peer review" meeting icon. The frustration icon next to the meeting icon represents the mood in the room when everybody realized they were working with the wrong sizing case.

b) Is related to the "prepare and present updates" activity, this time around being represented for each change management meeting, as there were two meetings in the respective time period, and they happened outside of the iterations. Please note how isolated they are; there's no push arrow linking them to other activities.

c) There's a new activity "determine and send attachment stiffness," performed by MECH, as a direct consequence of the new sizing case. This means the use of a new model represented in the information flow as the ATCH software icon.

d) The political aspect is represented by the discussion icon, with the text "bonus is tied to the on-time release." This becomes a trigger for chasing "need to deliver on time" (see the information path to the chase the chaser icon) and for declaring "draft released on time" (see the information path to the meeting icon), even though the release didn't include all the necessary cases (see the cloud icon "incomplete set of cases"; for the entire Sheet 3 please see Appendix C3).

Please continue mapping the narration. Ted continues:

We started immediately working on the second case, the "fully operative case," confident that since we've passed the sizing case, the rest will be easier. Unfortunately, that was not the case. We were spinning our wheels between "fail," chases and meetings for about two weeks, conscious about the fact that the mold started to be fabricated and the supplier needed to be informed as soon as possible of the changes, when the most senior "FSAF" specialist returned from sick leave and some frustrated senior management mandated an emergency meeting with her. That meeting was very instructive; I was glad to be part of it. After a brief introduction that included the analysis results and some related questions, the meeting soon became a university course, where the discussions went deep down into the physics of the phenomenon. All the data we've accumulated so far now interpreted by the most senior "FSAF" specialist was pointing toward something we've ignored until then: the frame to which the component was attached. Again, this was something we didn't have to consider in previous product designs but was induced by the ambitious new product requirements. The implications were huge: the "FSAF" analysis needed to include the whole assembly, not just the component. That meant possible modifications to the frame, not just to the component or to the attachment, opening much of the design space at a moment when metal needed to be cut if we were to finish on time. Back to square one. It was November 29. … At this point, the formal change management process kicked in and programs started to be even more involved, as there were weekly change management gover- nance meetings extra to the risk ones, and we were now required to use the change management repository under their guidance.

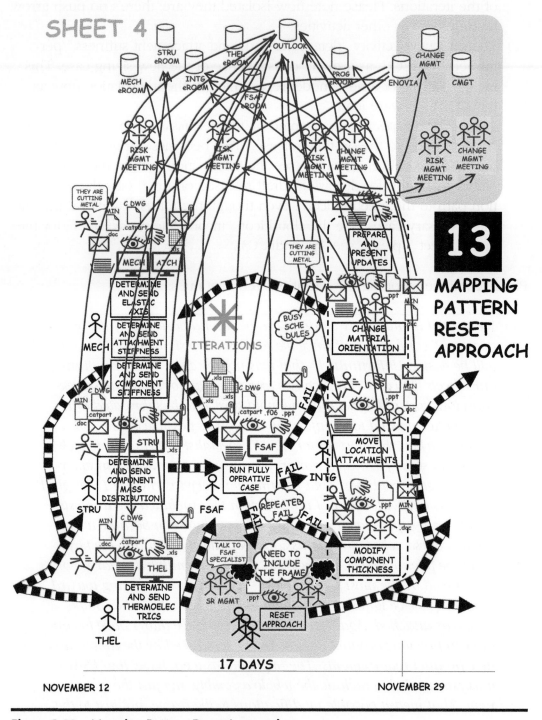

Figure 3.32 Mapping Pattern Reset Approach.

CHECKPOINT: So, how did you capture the narration? Here's a suggested view (see Figure 3.32). Please notice the "reset approach" activity. It's performed by a group of people, represented by the black ink three people icons. Its information flow includes the trigger, represented by the senior management meeting icon "talk to FSAF specialist," the input represented by the ".ppt" file icon, the enablers represented by the check icon and the meeting icon. The frustration is captured by the dark cloud and the major issue is represented by the "need to include the frame" cloud icon. Related to this activity, we can see that it is linked to the iterations by the push arrow with "fail" on it, so there's no "pass" for this cycle of iterations.

In the overall information flow, there are new additions: another governance meeting, represented by the weekly change management meeting icon, the "change management" database icon and the "they are cutting metal" chaser icon, meaning the execution urgency due to the mold fabrication already taking place.

Please continue mapping the narration. Ted continues:

> *Immediately, "MECH" determined the elastic axis and the stiffness of the assembly; "STRU" determined the mass distribution of the assembly; "THEL" determined the thermoelectrics. This time they all used the same .catproduct assembly drawing (including the component, attachment and frame) from ENOVIA and the minutes of the meeting detailing the modifications to do their work, and they all attached the .xls results files in their Outlook email messages to "FSAF." They performed the "attachment case," and after several iterations between chases, meetings, governance reports, all during the holiday season, we got a "pass." Once the pass was confirmed, we did some change impact assessment, but unfortunately, it was incomplete because the ones required to give us inputs were very slow to respond. What changed was the frame thickness and the component thickness. "DSGN" made the modifications in the .catproduct drawing while assessing the impacts of the frame thickness change. The changes went to the supplier January 7, even though the approval was not granted yet (FYI Mr. Supplier, changes are coming), almost two months after we claimed we released the requirements on time.*
>
> *We were working on the "fully operative case" when "CMGT," after revising the product configuration, called a meeting to validate the design assumptions, mainly related to material properties. All involved worked with the assumption that the frame material was the same as the component material, which proved to be false. This meant that the mass distribution was not represented correctly in the "FSAF" model, as "STRU" worked with the wrong assumption in their model. "STRU" made the necessary corrections on January 24 (end of story for Sheet 4).*

CHECKPOINT: So, how did you capture the narration? Here's a suggested view (see Figure 3.33). Please note how the parallelism of activities was captured. The activity "verify design assumptions" performed by CMGT is happening at the same time as the "push for next case" activity. While the latter is part of the stream of iteration-related activities, ending with the cloud icon "stop iteration," the first one is part of the validation-related activities, ending with the "modify STRU model" activity. The activities in both streams take place in the same time frame but are not linked to each other. The same is true for the "prepare and present updates" activity; as you will notice, it's not linked to any other activities by a push arrow (for the entire Sheet 4, please see Appendix C4).

Please continue mapping the narration. Ted continues:

"FSAF" went back to run again the "attachment case" with the corrected model results. Chases were required, as we were all conscious of the fact that the supplier started the mold fabrication. It took several iterations to get the "pass," while the frame thickness and the component thickness were changed again. This time we had consistent properties of the materials. Once the pass was confirmed, we did some change impact assessment, but again, it was incomplete because the ones required to give us inputs were very slow to respond. The changes went out on February 19 in an informal mode (FYI Mr. Supplier, changes are coming …), while the fabrication of the mold was progressing with what was deemed to have enough margins.

CHECKPOINT: So, how did you capture the narration? Did you include the weekly governance meetings? Have you added the extra activity for INTG called "assess change impacts"? Did you include the chaser "they are cutting metal"? Did you cover the triggers, inputs, enablers, outputs and info out? Please compare with the suggested view (see Figure 3.34).

Please continue mapping the narration. Ted continues:

While we were working on the "fully operative case," "MECH" realized that the attachment model "ATCH" didn't cover all the variability called by the "fully operative case," resulting in data that didn't make sense. Consequence: "MECH" needed to recalibrate the model "ATCH," and "FSAF" needed to run again the "attachment case." After the usual iterations involving frame and component thickness, attachment location and stiffness modifications, with the usual chases, meetings and governance reporting, we've sent the changes on March 11 to the supplier, again, in an informal way. As the numbers from impacts were adding up, it became obvious that all solutions involving the modification of the frame needed to be set aside because of the huge impact on recurring costs. Back to the drawing board … but before starting, senior management

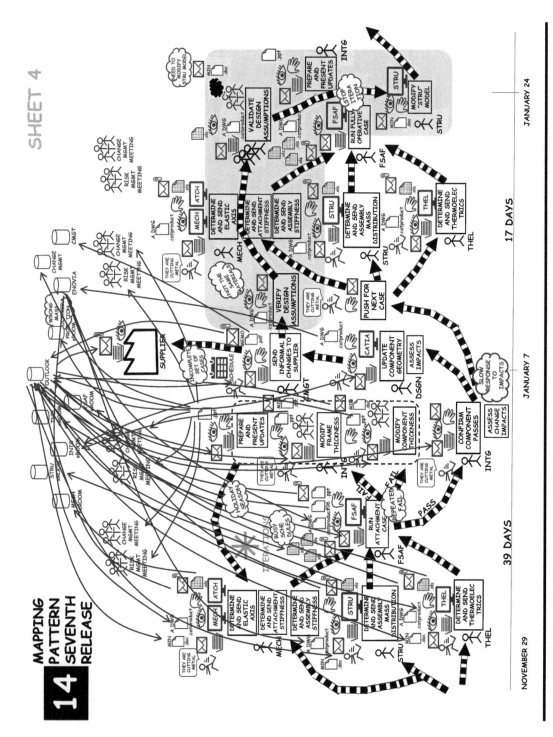

Figure 3.33 Mapping Pattern Seventh Release.

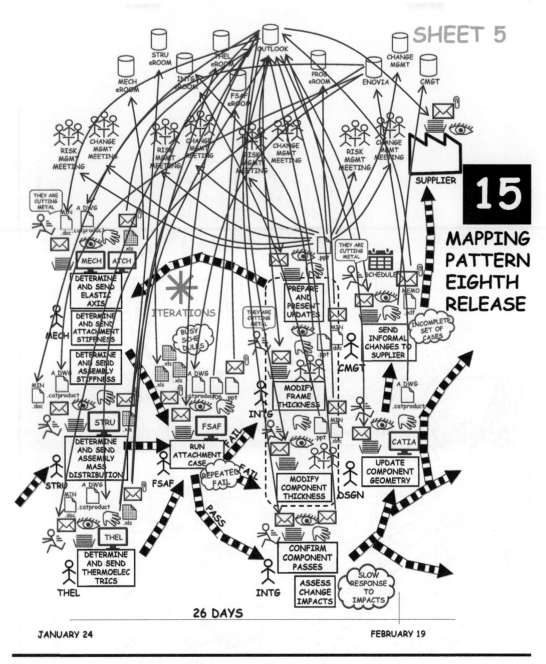

Figure 3.34   Mapping Pattern Eighth Release.

decided they need to align and support a new approach. What they did, they looked into the specialists' recommendations for a step approach covering all the technical aspects to be validated and verified; then they laid out a plan where all the engineering groups reporting to them got their priorities reconsidered, then committed to the execution of the plan. It was March 16. That made a difference (end of story for Sheet 5).

CHECKPOINT: So, how did you capture the narration? Here's a suggested view (see Figure 3.35). Please notice how the parallel activities "recalibrate

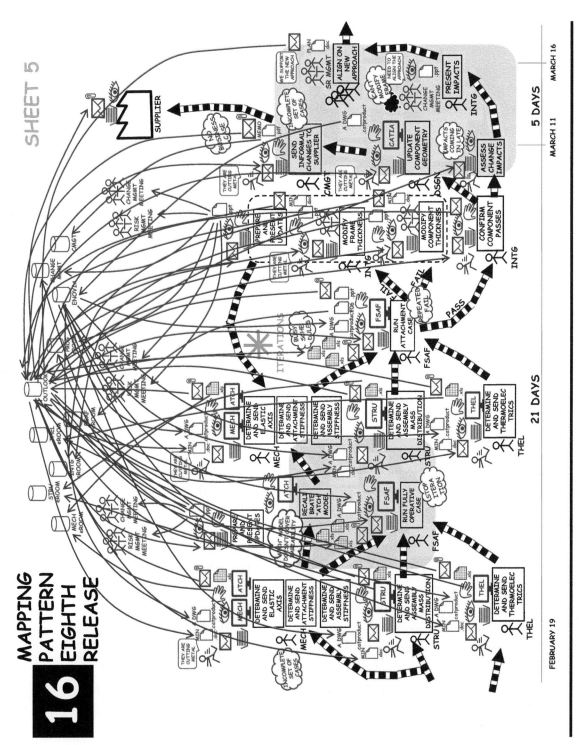

Figure 3.35   Mapping Pattern Eighth Release – Continued.

ATCH model" performed by MECH and "run fully operative case" performed by FSAF were captured. The first activity continues the flow of activities through the push arrow, while the latter activity ends without flow but in the cloud icon "stop iteration." The other two activities flow branches running in parallel start with the "confirm component passes" performed by INTG, with the first branch leading to the supplier icon, the second branch leading to the "align on new approach" activity icon performed by senior management. As you can see, the information flow for the "present impacts" activity performed by INTG includes the trigger represented by the meeting icon, the enabler represented by the ".ppt" file icon and the check icon, the output represented by the callout icon "need to align the approach," which becomes an automatic trigger for the "align on new approach" activity. The issue of "can't modify frame" and the frustration complete the information flow. The "align on new approach" activity is performed by a group of people represented by several black ink people icons, and its information flow includes the enabler represented by the meeting icon, the output represented by the callout icon "we support the new approach" and the ".ppt" file icon with the plan, the info out represented by the email icon linked to the Outlook icon (for the entire Sheet 5, please see Appendix C5).

Please continue mapping the narration. Ted continues:

> *This time around, we started with a validation of all models we were using, reviewing the compatibility between them, along with revising the entire set of design assumptions. We, "INTG," chaired the meetings and had "MECH," "STRU," "THEL," "FSAF" sitting at the same table with us and going over their methodologies, using real data to spot potential issues. Then, under the "FSAF" senior specialist's guidance, we dressed a common plan around the clear objective of not modifying the frame, specifying all the possible paths that were technically feasible.*
>
> *Using the assembly ".catproduct" drawing and the minutes of the meeting detailing the modifications as a starting point, we worked on the "attachment case," going through several iterations regarding the component thickness and attachment stiffness, this time without having to chase people. After several "fails," we realized that the only way this could work is to reduce the size of the component. There was no impact to the frame or to product performance, but it was enough to offset the component design and to require a new mold design. When we got the "pass," I immediately went to see Frank, and we had the discussion captured at the beginning of Chapter 1. Next thing, they called the supplier and told them to stop the fabrication of the mold. It was March 25.*

CHECKPOINT: So, how did you capture the narration? Here's a suggested view (see Figure 3.36). Please notice how several activities were captured in one, called "validate compatibility of models and design assumptions"

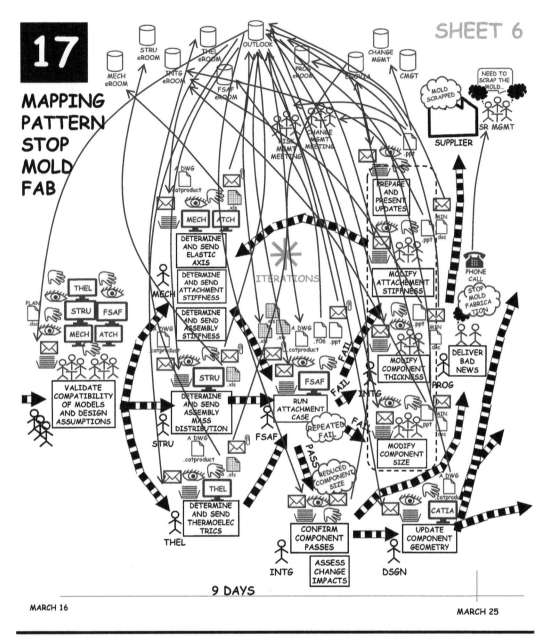

Figure 3.36   Mapping Pattern Stop Mold Fabrication.

performed by a group of people. This was done having in mind the relative duration of these activities (days) versus the total duration of the project (years), so for this application, compressing is justified, but it might be possible in other applications, where the total duration is shorter, to have to map each activity separately. The corresponding information flow actually shows several meeting icons as an enabler. The trigger is the email icon coming from the Outlook icon and the ".doc" document called "plan." The other enablers are the data manipulation icons and check icons; the inputs and outputs are the software icons corresponding to the models used by each specialized engineering function.

Please continue mapping the narration. Ted continues:

> *We continued with our plan and pursued the "fully operative case" between iteration work, governance presentations and updates in the change management software, without having to chase people, as the players were aligned due to the senior management setting the right priorities. We were just executing to the alignment plan. With the reduced size, we had to make just small thickness adjustments to the component to have the "pass" on April 2. The same thing happened with the "end of life case," but this time we needed to adjust the attachment's stiffness, and we were good. The change approval went smoothly, and the supplier got the memo the next day. It was April 9. Almost five months later than scheduled* (end of story Sheet 6).

CHECKPOINT: So, how did you capture the narration? Here's a suggested view (see Figure 3.37). How did you represent the change approval? Did you cover the triggers, inputs, enablers, outputs and info out (for the entire Sheet 6, please see Appendix C6).

If we're looking back to Figure 3.2, we notice that until now we've covered (a) the mapping pattern and (b) the time line. What's missing to complete the current state value stream map is adding (c) the cause and adverse effect, the rework and important blue ink markings.

It is suggested to start with cause and adverse effect, more precisely with the adverse effect itself, because it's easier to spot it. As a reminder, the adverse effect is represented with the boom icon, with a distinctive number on it. Let's start placing them on the map using Appendix C1 to C6.

The first adverse effect corresponds to this part of the story: *"The memo went out May 1. … About one week later we got a meeting invite from the 'FSAF' specialist. It was about a finding they made: the elastic axis in their model 'FSAF' was incorrectly represented because of the meshing differences with the 'MECH' model."* Here we have the realization that until then, they had worked with the wrong elastic axis. So, in Appendix C1, on the right side of the map, there's the "correct meshing mismatch" activity performed by FSAF. This is where the "Boom 1" icon belongs. To retrace its recorded cause, we need to go back and see where the FSAF model was used the first time because the meshing differences were supposed to be reconciled at that time. So, we place the "Time Bomb 1" icon next to the "run fully operative case" activity icon.

The second adverse effect corresponds to this part of the story: *"The memo went out June 19, and we had to shift our attention to other priorities … about one week later we got another meeting invitation from 'FSAF.' They were accompanied by 'THEL' … this time around it was the*

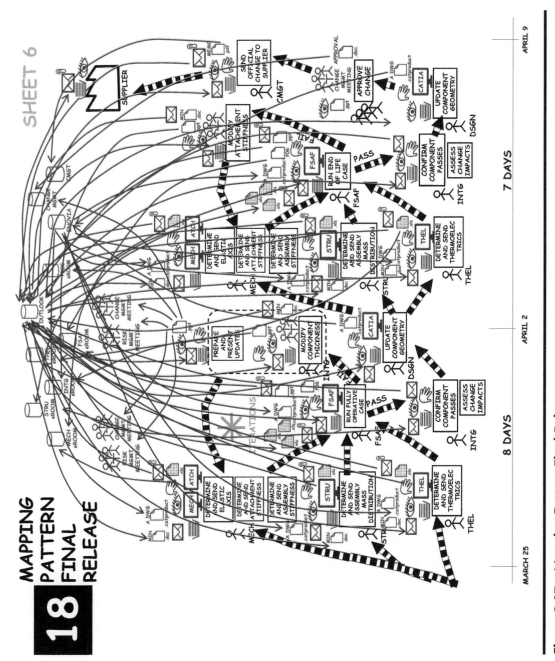

Figure 3.37   Mapping Pattern Final Release.

thermoelectric distribution in the 'FSAF' model wrongly represented due to a meshing error in the 'THEL' model." Here we have the realization that until then, they worked with the wrong thermoelectric distribution. So, the "Boom 2" icon is placed next to "correct meshing mismatch" activity performed by THEL in Appendix C2. Its cause is related to the first use of the THEL model, where the meshing was supposed to be verified and validated, so the "Time Bomb 2" icon belongs next to the "determine and send thermoelectrics" activity performed by THEL at the beginning of Appendix C1.

The third adverse effect corresponds to this part of the story: *"During the scheduled design peer review with engineering specialists from another new development program, it became apparent that we were working with the wrong sizing case. Because of the severe conditions the component was exposed to (never encountered by our other products), the sizing case was not the 'fully operative case' but the 'attachment case.' The implication was we needed to run now three cases instead of two. Back to square one. It was October 11."* Here we have the realization that until then they used the wrong sizing case. The "Boom 3" icon belongs then next to the "review design" activity performed by the group of people in Appendix C3. The corresponding "Time Bomb 3" icon belongs where all should have started with the right sizing case, next to the "run fully operative case" activity performed by FSAF in Appendix C1.

The fourth adverse effect corresponds to this part of the story: *"The most senior 'FSAF' specialist returned from sick leave, and some frustrated senior management mandated an emergency meeting with her … something we've ignored until then: the frame to which the component was attached. … The implications were huge: the 'FSAF' analysis needed to include the whole assembly, not just the component. That meant possible modifications to the frame, not just to the component or to the attachment, opening much of the design space at a moment when metal needed to be cut if we were to finish on time. Back to square one. It was November 29."* Here we have the realization that until then, they were using the wrong levers to secure a safe component design. Then the "Boom 4" icon belongs next to the "reset approach" icon performed by the group of people in Appendix C4. Consequently, the "Time Bomb 4" icon belongs next to the first group of iteration-related activities surrounded by the dotted line box in Appendix C1, where modifications of the whole assembly should have been considered in the first place.

The fifth adverse effect corresponds to this part of the story: *"All involved worked with the assumption that the frame material was the same as the component material, which proved to be false. This meant that the mass distribution was not represented correctly in the 'FSAF' model, as 'STRU' worked with the wrong assumption in their model. 'STRU' made the necessary corrections on January 24."* Here we have the realization that since the new approach started, they were working with the wrong design assumption involving the frame material. The "Time Bomb 5" icon belongs then next to the "determine and send mass distribution" activity performed by STRU, right after resetting the approach, in Appendix 4, where the right materials should have been used.

The sixth adverse effect corresponds to this part of the story: *"After February 19 … while we were working on the 'fully operative case,' 'MECH' realized that the attachment model 'ATCH' didn't cover all the variability called by the 'fully operative case,' resulting in data that didn't make sense,"* that can be found in Sheet 5, Appendix C5. Here we have the realization that they worked with a wrongly calibrated ATCH model until now. The "Boom 6" icon belongs next to the software icon representing the ATCH model used during the iteration work that revealed that it doesn't cover the variability and needed to be recalibrated. The corresponding "Time Bomb 6" icon is traced to the first use of the ATCH model, where the recalibration should have been done in the first place in Appendix C3, next to the software icon representing the ATCH model.

The seventh adverse effect corresponds to this part of the story: *"After March 11 … as the numbers from impacts were adding up, it became obvious that all solutions involving the modification of the frame needed to be set aside because of the huge impact on recurring costs."* Here we have the realization that it is too costly to modify the frame. Consequently, the "Boom 7" icon belongs next to the "present impacts" activity performed by INTG on Sheet 5, Appendix C5. The corresponding "Time Bomb 7" icon belongs where the change impacts started to be assessed but were incomplete because of the slow response from the ones required to give inputs in Appendix C4 next to the "assess change impacts" activity performed by INTG.

The eighth adverse effect corresponds to this part of the story: *"After several 'fails,' we realized that the only way this could work is to reduce the size of the component. There was no impact to the frame or to product performance, but it was enough to offset the component design and to require a new mold design. … Next thing, they called the supplier and told them to stop the fabrication of the mold. It was March 25."* Here we have the realization that the corresponding dimensions of a safe component design require scrapping the current, very expensive mold the supplier was working on. So, the "Boom 8" icon belongs next to the "deliver bad news" activity performed by PROG in Appendix C6. The "Time Bomb 8" icon can be positioned next to the "on-time" release of the requirements that were used to start mold fabrication in Appendix C3. These requirements were sent without "pass" from all the required cases before the approach was reset to cover working on the assembly.

With the adverse effects identified on the map, it is easier now to place the rework icons. Please place the rework icons on the maps you drew and then compare them with Appendix C:

The "rework 1" icon can be placed next to the "correct meshing mismatch" activity performed by FSAF in Appendix C1. The "rework 2" icon can be placed next to the "correct meshing mismatch" activity performed by THEL in Appendix C2. The "rework 3" icon can be placed next to "modify and validate FSAF model" performed by FSAF in Appendix C3. "Determine and send assembly stiffness" performed by MECH is the activity that replaces the "determine and send component stiffness" and represents an approach rework, so the "rework 4" icon belongs next to it in Appendix C4. The "rework 5" icon belongs next to the "modify STRU model" performed by STRU in Appendix C4. "Recalibrate ATCH model" performed by MECH in Appendix C5 is a rework activity, so the "rework 6" icon belongs next to it. "Modify component size" performed by INTG in Appendix C6 is the activity where the component size is used as a new lever, constituting an approach rework, so the "rework 7" icon belongs next to it. Finally, the "rework 8" icon belongs next to the supplier and represents the rework of the mold in Appendix C6. The rework summary table can be found in Appendix D3.

Once the cause and adverse effects and the rework are captured, we can make some blue markings on the map to highlight some key points. For example, we can use the turning point icon to highlight the activities that significantly influenced the course of the project in a positive way. One of them could be the meeting with the FSAF senior specialist who just returned from sick leave, the turning point being the opening of the design space by considering the entire assembly for the component design and resetting the approach, as captured in Appendix C4. This helped in finding the right levers for iteration work, ending with a safe component design. Another one could be the senior management alignment on the new approach, where they all determined, agreed and committed to the steps to follow, including resetting priorities for the different groups, as captured in Appendix C5. This greatly helped smooth execution.

3.6 Generic Considerations

When looking at the map captured in Appendix C1 to C6, please note several generic considerations:

■ The transition between sheets is made through unfinished push arrows at the right side that repeat on the left side of the next sheet.

■ Looking at the information flow on each sheet, you'll see two clusters of the same databases linked with their respective information paths. This choice was made to facilitate the reading of the illustrations as the story was captured; in a workshop environment, it is better to keep a single database icon for the whole map and draw the information paths accordingly.

■ Each information path is distinctive and links two information flow components. Please avoid collector-type information paths (see Figure 3.38). The same goes for group icons. Please don't try to over-simplify; this will greatly influence the overall visual impact in a negative way.

■ Don't get overwhelmed by the abundance of the information captured: let the activities' flow guide you through the stages, looking at the sequence captured through the push lines. Let the rework and cause and adverse effects icons show you the biggest pain points and the

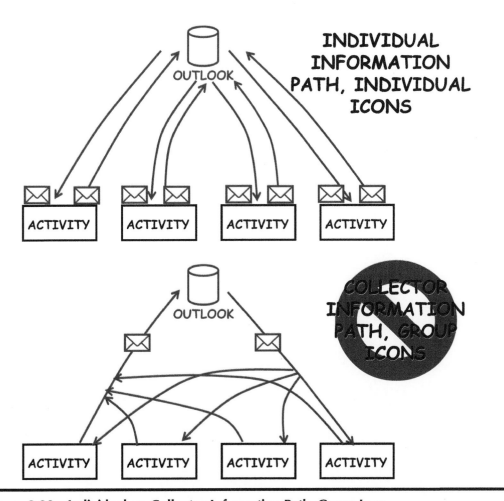

Figure 3.38 Individual vs. Collector Information Path, Group Icon.

turning point icons show you the helpful, positive shifts. Then you can get into the details of the specific information flow elements for a certain activity.

Well, congratulations, we've captured the current state. One can get quickly overwhelmed by looking at Appendix C1 to C6, but this is it; reality is messy in tangled environments and we must represent it as it is. We've just finished the first step in understanding what goes on. Now it's time for step two: trying to make sense out of it.

Chapter 4

Now That We Made It Visible, What Do We See?

You can surely appreciate the map you've drawn. Now we need to make the most of what we've captured. As you can see in Appendix C1 to C6, these current state value stream maps look really busy, are packed with a lot of information, so we need a way to make sense of them. The main reason we've drawn the current state this way is to be able to identify the waste and the failure modes. But what is waste? And why is it important to identify it?

4.1 What Is Waste and Why Care about It?

Waste is anything extra to what real work requires. Real work is work done for a real customer who buys the product or the service. Real work consists of continuously transforming the product or the service from the demand until it gets in the hand of the customer. Whatever makes it such that the continuous transformation of the product stops, is delayed or there's more activity than the transformation requires, is waste. We might transport the product from one workstation to another workstation; transporting it does not actually transform the product, so it's waste. We might upload a 100 MB file from ENOVIA and wait one hour to be able to start working on it; waiting for the file to upload does not actually transform the product, so it's waste. Being forced to correct meshing errors constitutes repair work, which is more activity than the transformation of the product requires, so it's waste. We might be in a governance meeting and give status about a project, but just giving status does not actually transform the project, so it's waste. Building products to a forecast is not building products for real customers, so it's waste. Developing products that customers don't actually buy is not developing products for real customers, so it's waste.

DOI: 10.4324/9781003050377-4

Waste is the main obstacle to on-time delivery, to high quality and to low costs. More waste in our processes translates into longer lead times for delivering the product. At the same time, more waste translates into higher defects rates and rework, which then translates into higher costs and lost business opportunities. Removing this obstacle is key to profitability and growth. However, waste removal by itself cannot be done unless we identify the waste first. The challenge of the multifunctional environments where the product is hard to see and the work is nonrepetitive is that waste is not visible by direct observation. We might enter an open office space with hundreds of people, everyone looking very busy, some of them wearing headphones and having heated discussions over video conferences, some of them manipulating complicated 3D schematics on their screens, others exploring spreadsheets with thousands of lines – but how do we differentiate between product transformation and waste by what we see? Without a context, it's impossible. The context is given by the real case we've mapped, so capturing the current state value stream map is the first step to identifying the waste.

For ease of identification, waste was categorized into several types, but, of course, there are more. The types of waste widely publicized are, in no particular order, waiting, inventory, defects, overprocessing, overproduction, motion, transportation and unused talent. Please note that these are things or activities, ***people are never waste***. You can find some examples of waste in tangled environments in Table 4.1

Table 4.1   Examples of Waste in Tangled Environments

Type	Why	Examples
Waiting Product's state of inactivity	While waiting, the product is not transformed	• No response to emails • Management approvals • Signature cycles • Expert approvals • Information created too early (won't be processed in the immediate future) • Information created too late • Not attended meetings, needing rescheduling • Excessive buy-in and alignment time • Licenses not available • Waiting to upload or download • Endless debates with no conclusions • Seeking absolute consensus for decisions/decisions by committee • Not aligned priorities • Printing lineup

(Continued)

Table 4.1 (*Continued*)   Examples of Waste in Tangled Environments

Type	Why	Examples
Defects Product's characteristic of not meeting specifications or needs	Defects require repair and trigger extra transformation work. Rework does not transform the product; it repairs something that should have been done right in the first place	• Reworked analysis and drawings • Important details omitted • Ppt presentations where the "not important" prevails and the "important" is not seen • Wrong/incomplete info passed on • Wrong assumptions used • Missing stakeholders • Unclear decision • Reversed decision • Multiple, conflicting priorities • Analysis wrongly done • Conversion error • Excessive synthesis – not really representing the facts, not actionable
Inventory Product's unfinished state or required inputs' state of sitting idle between or at the transformation steps	While in inventory, the product or its components are not transformed	• Accumulation of documents to be processed • Unread emails • Excessive non-necessary data • Full inboxes • Too many databases • Large ppts (lots of slides) • Large to-do lists • Large models (CATIA)
Overproduction Producing more than actually needed by the customer	Producing more than is needed ties effort that is not available to transform what is really needed	• Same info presented in different formats • Duplicated files for the same item • Ppt presentations where the "not important" slides prevail • Too many cc's on emails • Too many KPIs • Too many slides for a particular item • Too many email exchanges on the same topic
Transportation Product's state of being transported	While being transported, the product is not transformed	• Off-site meetings • Email attachments • Handoff paper documents • Automated workflows

(Continued)

Table 4.1 (*Continued*) Examples of Waste in Tangled Environments

Type	Why	Examples
Overprocessing Product's state of being processed more than its required, effort-wise or technical detail–wise	More processing than required slows down the necessary product transformation and ties extra effort	• "Reinventing the wheel" • Excessive governance/reporting • Excessive deliverables for the same outcome • Too many meetings to conclude/advance • Too much verification/validation • Too many activities and documents for a decision • Too many different forms of status/changes • Rewriting already existing documents • Too many iterations • Unnecessary data conversions • Too much detail • Info spread in too many different locations • Perfectionism "polishing the apple" • Excessive clip art • Too many buttons to click/check-in info systems • Excessive convergence between different stakeholders • "Embarking" leadership • Overlapping Roles & Responsibilities • Excessive consultation • Excessive handoffs • Several lists to track the same thing
Movement Being in motion state of the one transforming the product	While being moved, the product is not transformed	• Getting prints from the printer • Chasing people at their desks • Mouse clicks • Searching for stuff • Too many redundant meetings
Unused talent State of the one transforming the product of not being allowed to perform at its full potential	Losing people's motivation and creativity slows down the product transformation	• Chasers • Highly qualified people used for underqualified jobs • Discarding people's ideas • Prevailing office politics

Now that we've learned what waste is and why we should care about it, we need to use this information and find ways to qualify and quantify waste in the captured current state VSM. The question then becomes, What in the current state value stream map reveals waste?

4.2 What Reveals Waste?

4.2.1 VSM Icons Reveal Waste

When qualifying waste, the first thing to do is to look at the icons captured in the current state map and associate them with types of waste.

Let's take, for instance, the inbox icon. With what type of waste can we associate it? The most obvious would be inventory (see Figure 4.1–5). In the multifunctional environment where the product is hard to see, and the work is nonrepetitive, it is not uncommon for people to receive over 200 emails daily. No matter how much effort these people put into responding, it is not realistic to assume they will clear their inboxes by the end of the day. These emails contain information that accumulates – the key word here being *accumulates*. Accumulation is tightly linked to creating inventory. Another thing accumulation is tightly linked to is waiting (see Figure 4.1–1). As the emails are not responded to, the information regarding a product's transformation does not reach the ones needing it, so the product is not transformed.

The information flow icons involving people are interesting cases. As we saw earlier, *people are never waste*; then why do we associate the people-related icons with waste? Let's dive into the subject, case by case:

The people information icon – if a person verbally distributing jobs to others is sick, the jobs are not performed because there was no other means to vehiculate the information, with the consequence of the product not being transformed (see Figure 4.1–1). This is not about the person but about the situation, so in this case, we can associate the situation with the waste

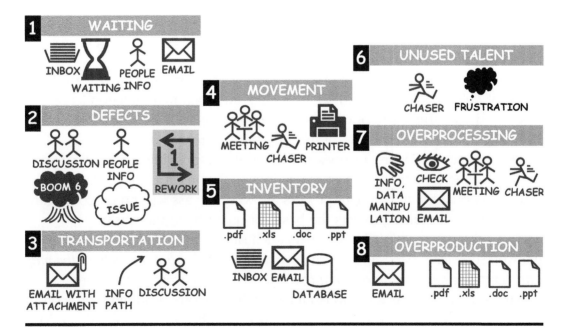

Figure 4.1   VSM Icons That Reveal Waste.

of waiting. The same is true for defects (see Figure 4.1–2). If the only way to transmit information is through a person, and if for various reasons the information is interpreted and passed on the wrong way by that person, the product is transformed with the wrong information and defects are generated. Consequently, in both cases, *people are not waste*; the situation of relying just on people to vehiculate important information is. So, the people information icon reveals a potential for waste of waiting and defects.

We can say the same for the chaser icon. The situation of chasing people for information or for deliverables can be associated with several types of waste: movement (see Figure 4.1–4), as sometimes this implies walking to different buildings, floors; overprocessing (see Figure 4.1–2), as looking for information means spending more effort than one should. The clearest association though is with the waste of unused talent (see Figure 4.1–6). It is rather unrewarding for very qualified professionals to spend the entire working day chasing people, asking, "Where is the report? It was supposed to be delivered last week?" "When will you be able to deliver the memo, we can't do anything without it?" "Where can I find last year's test results. I've searched everywhere, but I'm not able to find them?" "We're stuck. Who else can help me find the analysis results?" So, while the chasing is going on, the person doing it cannot transform the product, with the hidden consequences of the person's morale going down and his or her frustration going up.

Other people-related icons revealing waste: the discussion icon can be associated with the waste of defects (see Figure 4.1–2) and transportation (see Figure 4.1–3) as information is passed from one person to another, leaving the door open to interpretation. Again, it is the situation of discussion between people being the only way of passing – or we can say transporting – relevant information. The meeting icon can be associated with the waste of overprocessing (see Figure 4.1–7) because meetings can be redundant; movement (see Figure 4.1–4) because this could mean walking to different buildings, floors, searching for conference rooms; and even waiting if product transformation is pending on a meeting outcome.

Some icons are self-explanatory, like the rework icon associated with the waste of defects (see Figure 4.1–2), the check and data manipulation icons associated with the waste of overprocessing (see Figure 4.1–7) or the waiting icon associated with the waste of waiting (see Figure 4.1–1).

Please note that Figure 4.1 does not cover all the possibilities, as we've seen in the meeting icon case, but just the main associations; it is for guidance only. What's important is the thought process allowing the association of icons with types of waste because this sets the basis for quantifying the waste.

To facilitate quantifying the waste, there's a simple but important activity that the workshop team needs to perform: *counting the individual icons from the map and compiling the result in a summary.* You can see an example in Figure 4.2:

This can be done as a group exercise, with someone picking up an icon and then counting the number of occurrences for that icon, while others do

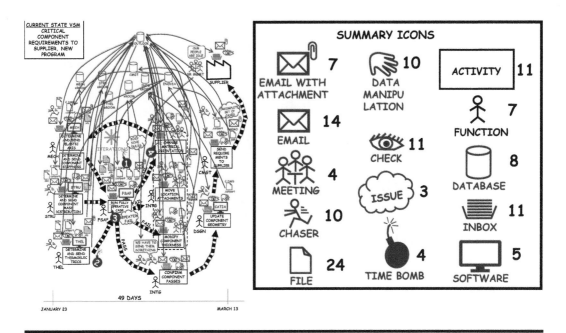

Figure 4.2 Summary Icons for a Fragment of Current State VSM.

the same but for a different icon. As you notice, in Figure 4.2, the file icons were counted as a single category, regardless of the extension: ".xls," ".doc," ".catpart." At the same time, the chasing the chaser situation was counted as two icons. Please be aware that in the summary, we will always find *the minimum* number of occurrences. For example, we've counted four meeting icons, but as we see it, some belong to the iteration loop, so in reality, there were more than four meetings happening, but for simplification, we will state: "minimum four meetings." The same is true for the activity icons – as you can see, some belong to the iteration loop too. Finally, considering the level of granularity that was chosen, it is very safe to state that the count for all the icons in the table is a "minimum."

4.2.2 Information Flow Patterns Reveal Waste

Counting the number of icons and associating them to types of waste is straightforward and relatively easy to do, but there's more to discover when we look at the current state VSM. If we look closely, we can see patterns emerging. These patterns give excellent insights into the more intangible, hidden aspects, involving behaviors and organizational culture. Let's look at Figure 4.3 and walk through each pattern. Please note that not all the possible patterns are presented but the main ones – to be used for guidance.

The *people-to-people pattern* (see Figure 4.3–1) involves a people information icon that links with several activities through information path icons. The information path from the people information icon to the activity is usually an order to perform an activity, the information path from the

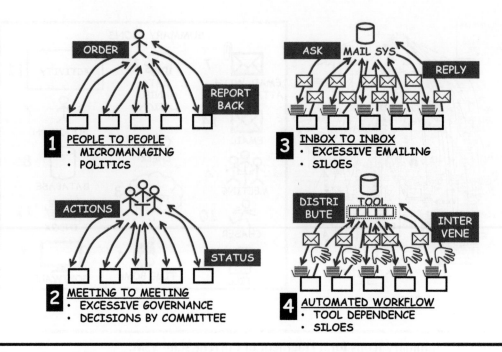

Figure 4.3   Information Flow Patterns – Link to Culture and Behaviors.

activity to the people information icon represents some sort of report back on how the activity was performed, but there are cases when the information path is only the order. In other words, this pattern represents situations when someone, usually in a management position, gives orders to one or several people to perform specific activities that might or might not be connected. A variant of this pattern could include the discussion icon instead of the people information icon. This pattern reveals cultural and behavioral aspects like micromanaging and organizational politics. According to Wikipedia, *micromanagement* is a management style whereby a manager closely observes and/or controls and/or reminds the work of his/her subordinates or employees and *organizational politics* could be defined as the use of power and social networking within an organization to achieve changes that benefit the organization or individuals within it. Both are related to waste. When micromanaging, the triggers to perform work, information related to work, decisions related to work are all dependent on a single person. If that person, for various reasons, is not around, the continuous transformation of the product is at risk. An even more damageable situation is when that person is controlling the information, makes decisions and triggers activities for his or her own benefit, not the product's benefit. The most obvious types of waste related to *people-to-people pattern* are: defects, overprocessing and waiting.

The *meeting-to-meeting* pattern (see Figure 4.3–2) is similar to the people-to-people pattern when the people information icon is replaced by the meeting icon. In this case, the information path from the meeting icon to the activity usually represents a list of action items, the information path from the activity to the meeting icon represents status, but there are cases when the information path is only the status. In other words, this pattern represents situations when work is managed through meetings. Meeting participants look at the status, most of the time ask questions and debate, sometimes make decisions, sometimes they action people to perform work. These actions might or might not be connected. This pattern reveals mostly cultural aspects like excessive governance and decision by committee. The intent of governance meetings for a big project is to give a structure to the whole process, to ensure that the project is aligned with business goals and stays on target, reducing the risk of failure. They can have different names, but all evolve around titles like project review, program review, change management review, risk review, design review. The "decision by committee" implies a decision-making approach relying on a group of stakeholders rather than on one person to make decisions, with the goal of fostering buy-in from the stakeholders by including their diverse perspectives when making the decisions. Although they both have positive aspects, we can relate them to waste. When work advancement is managed mainly through meetings, the continuous product transformation is always at risk. When, for instance, key players can't attend these meetings – which in big projects could be the norm – two alternatives are usually considered: continue work without the input from them or reschedule the meeting. Both alternatives are potentially damaging, by generating defects or by delaying work. When work advancement is heavily dependent on decisions that a group of people need to make, the continuous transformation of the product is at risk too. It is difficult to make timely decisions in an environment where you have a lot of strong characters expressing their opinions at once. When, for instance, 20 specialists in a room are trying to make a decision, no matter how long the meeting lasts, there's a high possibility that the decision is not going to be made because all of them bring very pertinent divergent points, so convergence toward a single answer is almost impossible. The most obvious types of waste we can relate to the meeting-to-meeting pattern are waiting and overprocessing.

The *inbox-to-inbox* pattern (see Figure 4.3–3) involves the electronic mail system (e.g., Outlook) icon that links with several activities and their respective inboxes through information path icons. The information path from the electronic mail system icon to the inbox icon is usually an email requesting some kind of action; the information path from the activity to the electronic mail system icon represents a reply email, but there are cases when the information path is only the request (not responding emails). In other words, this pattern represents situations where work is managed through emails. This pattern reveals cultural and behavioral aspects like excessive emailing and organizational silos. Excessive emailing denotes a mindset of using mostly emails when communicating with other people. The emails' content varies but evolves around certain categories like asking for status, asking for information, pushing information, asking to perform work, pushing work, following up, FYI (for your info) or CC (carbon copy). Organizational silos describe the isolation of certain groups that occurs within a company. Typically, an organizational silo is based on a rigid organizational structure, has its own goals and priorities and has a mentality of driving results to achieve the silo's goals no matter what and involves a strong sense of belonging for the people within. As a rule of thumb is the bigger the company and more geographically dispersed, the greater the number of silos composing it. The preferred inter-silo communication vehicle is email. When most of the work is managed by emails, the continuous transformation of the product is at risk. Two aspects: first, is the pile of emails accumulating in the inbox, second is the required back and forth to solve complicated matters. As we've seen previously, the accumulation can be associated with the inventory and waiting types of waste – see Figure 4.1 and the related discussion around the inbox icon. In order to solve complicated matters in the tangled environment, it is not unusual for an email thread to have a running list of over 30 emails in it, and, of course, there might be a lot of email threads – this can be associated mainly with waiting, overprocessing and overproduction types of waste (see the email icon in Figure 4.1). The inbox-to-inbox pattern can be associated with the four aforementioned types of waste.

The *automated workflow* pattern (see Figure 4.3–4) involves a database icon that links with several activities and their respective inboxes through information path icons. The database icon is used for simplification reasons; in this case, it represents an automated workflow system linked to the electronic mail system. The information path from the database icon to the inbox icon is usually an email distributing tasks or status, the information path from the activity to the database icon represents some sort of manual intervention that needs to be done in the screens of the automated workflow. Depending on the type of automated workflow system, the manual intervention can be done with or without the task distribution email. In other words, this pattern represents situations when work is managed by the automated workflow system. This pattern reveals behavioral and cultural aspects like excessive tool dependence and organizational silos. The excessive tool dependence reflects a mindset of performing work just when the tool distributes the task. As tasks are aligned by specialty in the automated workflow system, this situation reinforces the silo mentality of working in isolation. When most of the work is managed by an automated workflow, the continuous transformation of the product is at risk, mostly related to the reception of the task distributed by the system. Beyond the accumulation of emails in the inbox, there's another potential danger: the emails sent from the system have generic titles; the emails need to be opened to see the details. When someone receives 20 notifications from the system daily, 19 of them being about status and 1 asking for a task to be performed, there's a high possibility that the person disregards all the messages coming from the system. This means disregarding the task, so the work is not performed, which delays the transformation of the product. The most obvious type of waste that is associated with the automated workflow pattern is waiting.

Figuring out what information flow patterns are prevalent in the current state VSM is an important step because beyond exposing waste, it exposes the prevalent behaviors and organizational culture elements that need to be corrected by the future state.

4.3 Need to Dig Deeper?

The first level of capturing failure modes in the current state VSM is through the rework table (see Appendix D3) and through the cause and adverse effect summary table (see Appendix D2), where we recorded all the time bomb and boom icons with the corresponding details of the adverse effect, the visible cause and the impacts. We can call them the visible failure modes, as they happened in the real case and are directly identified on the map. This table can be supplemented to include potential failure modes, failures that didn't occur in the real case, but there's a fair possibility of occurrence by the way the current process is laid out. This can be done by looking at the current state VSM, identifying the weak process points and filling a two-column table with the "IF – THEN" headers. In the IF column, we record the weak point as a condition, and in the THEN column, we record the obvious consequence in the case the condition materializes. For example, if the process weak point is identified as "standards reinforcement," in the IF column, we capture the condition of "standards use not reinforced," and in the THEN column, we capture the consequence of "possible design rework." A third column could be added to include the potential impacts, in the aforementioned example, there could be "delays." Capturing the failure modes is important because the setup of the future state should prevent their occurrence.

When the team identifies systemic issues by looking at the current state VSM, it might be necessary to go beyond just recording failure modes to performing root cause analysis. Sometimes a 5 Whys analysis is enough to expose the root causes, but there's a *big caution* that goes with how to perform it. As mentioned earlier, the root causes for poor process performance in multifunctional environments where the product is hard to see and the work is nonrepetitive are not easily identifiable due to numerous process activities, their hidden interdependencies and the multitude of stakeholders involved. One of the consequences is that the 5 Whys layout is not linear but looks like a tree (see Figure 4.4), with the problem statement at the top and lots of branches developing as we approach the root causes and with the number of layers going beyond five. These branches can be intertwined with common intermediary causes and sometimes lead to common root causes. Following the branches by asking why is dependent on how well the proximate causes were set at the beginning of the exercise, which of course is dependent on how well the problem was stated. Another consequence is the difficulty of bringing substantiation to the answers in the

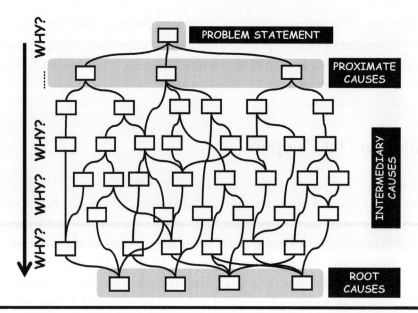

Figure 4.4 Typical Layout of a 5 Whys Exercise in Tangled Environments.

form of facts and data. These difficulties make it such that the exercise would be challenging to facilitate and consequently could take a lot of time.

4.4 Time to Step Back and Conclude

It is really interesting to see participants' reactions once the current state VSM is on the wall (or on the screen); the icons are counted; the prevalent information flow patterns are identified, along with the behavioral and cultural aspects; and the failure modes are summarized. By this time, the extent of the problem is obvious, so there are mixed feelings floating around: relief, as they understand now why their day-to-day is a struggle, and despair, as they realize how difficult it's going to be to correct it. Now the team is well equipped to perform the final part of the current state VSM, the conclusions.

The conclusions of the current state VSM are drawn by looking at the map and at the other materials and making objective statements about what the map and the other materials are revealing. The activity is led by the facilitator who writes the statements, making sure that everybody contributes. Here are some examples of statements:

- We have excessive governance, 57 status meetings identified.
- We are extremely busy, but we are not working on the right things.
- The worse it is, the more meetings are called.
- We work in silos.
- Defects and waiting are prevalent types of waste, see summary icons.
- We're in the meeting-to-meeting environment.

■ Decisions are not communicated clearly.
■ We have excessive chasing, 26 chasing situations identified.

These conclusions are very important because they become the basis for formulating the future state criteria.

4.5 Time to Practice

Please look at Figure 4.5 and answer the following questions:

1. What are the predominant icons, and what type of waste can they be associated with?
2. What information flow patterns do you see?
3. What behavioral and cultural elements do you see? Explain.
4. What prevalent types of waste do you see?

You can find the supporting materials and the conclusions for the current state value stream map in Ted's example in Appendix D.

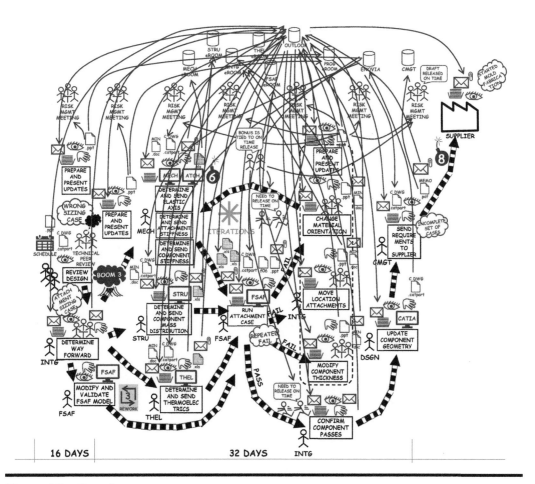

Figure 4.5 Exercise.

Chapter 5

Now That We Understand It, What Would We Like It to Be?

After spending a lot of effort, the team captured what happened, reaching the point when they finally concluded on the current state VSM. They are very proud of their achievement, and it's impossible not to notice it: they speak eloquently during the leadership reports out, bring in colleagues to show them the VSM, explaining the waste and the failure mechanisms. Their understanding of the whole situation grew exponentially during the exercise, and it shows. Their commitment to fix it is stronger than ever, but there are several obstacles that need to be overcome. The first obstacle becomes apparent as they look at the materials covering the walls of the conference rooms, scratching their heads and asking, "Now what?"

This is the moment when the facilitator needs to emphasize the steps that need to be taken to achieve the future state: establish the future state criteria, build a sound technical backbone, plan the waste removal, establish the future state strategy (see Figure 5.1).

5.1 Future State Criteria

The future state criteria (Figure 5.1–1) are a set of statements about what the future state needs to accomplish. The first goal of the criteria is to orient the thinking of the team in their effort to reshape the process, the second and most important goal is to prove the quality of the future state by checking it against the criteria. *Important note: the criteria is not about what the future state needs to look like but about what the future state needs to accomplish (no solutions in the criteria). For example: "need to have a visual board" is not a criterion, it is a means of achieving the criterion of "real-time visibility."* Please make sure that the objective given in the VSM exercise translates into items in the criteria. For instance, if the objective is "cut lead time in half," the criterion of "50% less lead time" needs to be captured.

DOI: 10.4324/9781003050377-5

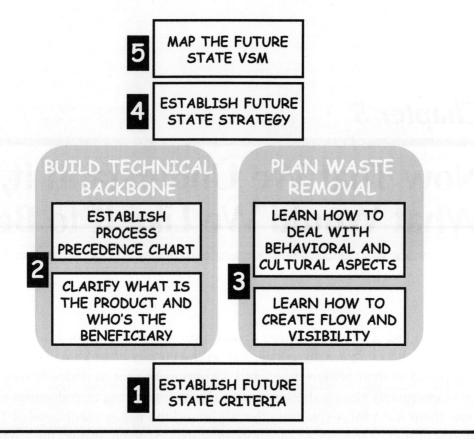

Figure 5.1   Steps to Reach the Future State VSM.

The criteria are derived from the current state VSM conclusion statements. If, for instance in the conclusions current state VSM we captured "*we have excessive chasing, 26 chasing situations identified*," the criteria for the future state should be something in line with "*no more chasing*." The *no more chasing* criterion will be used while designing the future state map by asking, "What new process step or other means would make sure we're not chasing anymore?" And when the future state is mapped, we ask, "What in this future state map prevents chasing?" Table 5.1 shows some derived criteria from the example statements in Chapter 4 (see "Time to Step Back and Conclude).

Once the derivations of criteria are made, there's a need to consolidate the list and bring it to a list of a maximum of eight to ten items. These consolidated items will constitute the future state VSM criteria. For example, in Table 5.1, from six current state statements, four criteria were consolidated (see the third column in the table): items 2, 3 and 5 were kept as such, while the items 1, 4 and 6 were consolidated in one single statement: "Less reliance on meetings and chasing to advance work." This statement includes by default the "50% less governance meetings" statement and then it is modified to include the "no more chasing" statement – see the addition underlined on statement 4.

Table 5.1   Derived Criteria from the Ted Example

Conclusions Current State VSM	*Criteria Future State VSM*	
We have excessive governance, 57 status meetings identified	~~50% less governance meetings~~	1
We work in silos	No more working in silos	2
Defects and waiting are prevalent types of waste, see summary icons	No defects, no waiting	3
We're in the meeting-to-meeting environment	Less reliance on meetings <u>and chasing</u> to advance work	4
Decisions are not communicated clearly	Decisions clearly communicated	5
We have excessive chasing, 26 chasing situations identified	~~No more chasing~~	6

5.1.1 Time to Practice

Please look at Appendix D4 and try to consolidate the future state VSM criteria and then answer the following questions:

■ How many items did you settle for in establishing the criteria?
■ What was the rationale behind your choice?

You can find the criteria for the future state VSM for Ted's story in Appendix E1.

5.2 Technical Backbone

The second step is to build a sound technical backbone (see Figure 5.1–2). What does this mean? It's going back to the fundamentals of what the process needs to achieve and how. The first part is the necessary clarification of what the product delivered by the process is and who benefits from it; the second part is going back to the essential process steps and their alignment against what the product needs in order to be transformed. What does it mean, *essential process steps*? It refers to the high-level activities required to transform the product, arranged in precedence order, excluding any activity that does not transform the product. For instance, if we take the product "drawing," the activity of "approve drawing" does not transform the product; the activity of "modify drawing" does. The first activity is touching the product, but is not transforming it.

Remember Denise, IT VP, and the IT project called eHOPE? This is what she was mentioning about figuring out what the product was during the workshop: "It took us a couple of hours just to figure out what was our product." Her conclusion? "And that was time well spent! Here's what we've come up with: *our product is a process incorporating best practices, supported by tools and implementation procedures.*" Concerning the beneficiary of the product, this is what Louis, engineering process and tools director, had to say. "The real challenge though," adds Louis,

> "was to make the link from our product to the paying customer. Let me explain: we deliver a process supported by tools, best practices and instructions to new product development teams, who will eventually use it to bring a new product to the market. Quite a stretch, no? What we realized while pushing the thought, is that by not delivering the required functionality, we contributed to the new product development process inefficiencies, translated into late delivery to the paying customer."

To summarize, the product for the eHOPE project is a process (not just software), and it benefits the new product development teams. The implications? The process steps required to transform the product need to cover more than writing code; they need to include establishing the process, establishing and incorporating the best practices associated with it, establishing and supporting implementation procedures associated with it; they need to include inputs from the new product development teams regarding their needs in order to do their work properly (see Figure 5.2–2).

The other implications reside in the roles and responsibilities of those involved in the development of the product. Denise explains:

> "Before [see Figure 5.2–1] it was IT Project Office's responsibility to issue a SOW (Statement Of Work), to define the WBS (Work Breakdown Structure) where the different groups were attributed specific work that then was tied together into a project plan. The

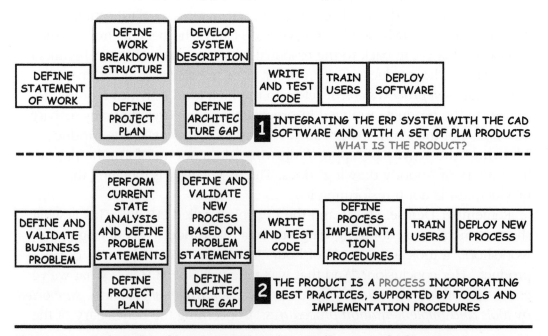

Figure 5.2 Technical Backbone, eHOPE Project, Before (1) and After (2).

specialized groups, like Data Management, Process & Tools, the software provider or the Solution Architect would do individually their part, the only instances they were linked was through governance, mainly the project reviews. This way of working was reinforcing the silo mentality of the stakeholders, fueling frustration along the way because of the difference of opinions on how to proceed. As they were defending their particular point of view, progress was slow and misguided, ending with late delivery and user frustration, as the delivered functionality didn't meet their needs.

Much changed in the After situation [see Figure 5.2–2], including roles and responsibilities. Work on new IT projects starts with defining and validating the business problem and is performed by the leadership team. It makes sense, they are the ones well positioned to know the business issues, the business priorities, the business trade-offs required. Once they've defined and validate the business problem, a multidisciplinary group of senior technical analysts, architects and business owners are looking into the current state surrounding the business problem (including architecture context and interdependencies) and derive clear problem statements that the solution needs to resolve, along with an initial, broad project plan. This is then taken by a dedicated multifunction team that goes into the details of identifying the solution, developing the detailed plan, developing and validating the solution, which involves writing and testing code, elaborating the implementation procedures and the training and implementation plan. This dedicated multifunction team includes new product development specialists, providing their input into the identification of the solution. Resources from the IT Project Office were redeployed in the multifunction teams, too. This new setting makes an unbelievable difference!"

5.2.1 Time to Practice

Please look at Figure 3.19 and at the future state VSM criteria in Appendix E1, and try to determine the technical backbone and then answer the following questions:

- What new activities did you propose, and what activities did you keep?
- What was the rationale behind your choice?

You can find the technical backbone for the future state VSM for Ted's story in Appendix E2.

5.3 The Waste Machine

Once the direction is set through the future state criteria and the new technical backbone is laid out, the second obstacle in front of the workshop team is: how to remove waste? As we saw in Chapter 4, waste is the main obstacle to on-time delivery, to high quality and to low costs. Removing this obstacle is key to profitability and growth. There's a two-step process in dealing with waste: (1) identify waste and (2) remove waste; in Chapter 4, we've learned ways of identifying waste, now it's time to learn about ways of removing waste.

But first, let's look into a concept that will help us better understand how waste works: The *Waste Machine* (see Figure 5.3). In the Waste Machine concept, we describe what this machine delivers, how the machine works and what fuels the machine. *Please note that this is a simplified model and incorporates just major contributors, not all contributors.*

The Waste Machine is more present than one would think, especially in tangled environments. There's a simple way to sense its presence: every time people complain, "We spend too much," "We are late," "We don't have enough resources," reflecting situations of cost overruns, late deliveries, quality problems reaching the customer, that's a good indication that the Waste Machine is there because that is exactly what the machine delivers (see Figure 5.3–1).

How does it work? The engine of the Waste Machine is constituted by the types of waste we've learned about in Chapter 4, not taken individually but feeding on each other like a complicated gear setting where they're all

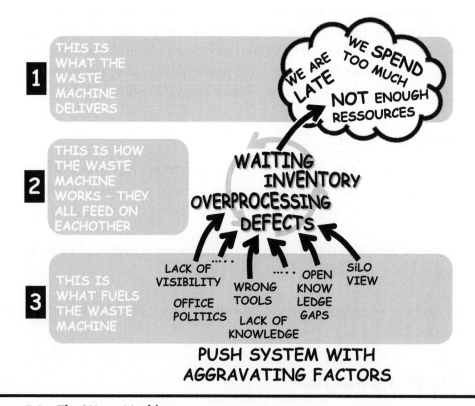

Figure 5.3 The Waste Machine.

intertwined (see Figure 5.3–2). Let's take an example: if there are wrong tolerances specified in a released drawing, this constitutes the defect type of waste. When the wrong tolerance defect is found, it requires some sort of rework, which means going back in the process and entering a queue of design jobs that need to be delivered, growing the number of jobs and creating the inventory type of waste. While in inventory, the drawing is not reworked, it waits, creating the waiting type of waste. But it doesn't stop here: it might be possible that changes will occur while the drawing is waiting, making the initial tolerancing considerations obsolete. If the drawing rework is done with the obsolete tolerancing considerations, it generates, again, defects, which then generate, again, inventory and waiting, ending as an overprocessing type of waste. If we're throwing in the mix the related clarification or chasing emails, the related meetings, transportation and movement type of waste is generated, which in turn create waiting. The outcome of this situation is late drawing delivery, resources overload and more associated costs. These intertwined intricacies make it hard to figure out how to remove waste. To have a better understanding, we need to dig deeper and look into what fuels the Waste Machine.

What fuels the Waste Machine? Fundamentally, it's the current system driving the work along with some aggravating factors (see Figure 5.3–3).

5.3.1 The Push System

The most widespread, fundamental system driving work in tangled environments is the *push system.* A push system is built on division of labor, where the product transformation relies on work being passed on between a multitude of very specialized functions until it gets into the hands of the paying customer. Sometimes it's called the "throw over the fence approach." The push system is disconnected from the real customer demand, transforming products based on forecast and projections vs. real-time demand and managing the delta by building otherwise unnecessary inventories. Because of its setup, *it guarantees that the product transformation happens with the longest lead times possible and guarantees that the product transformation accumulates the highest costs possible.* With a push system, the norm is that the customer receives the product late and with defects, while the business struggles with cash flow and profit.

A by-product of the push system is the *silo mentality or view,* where the interests of the silo have precedence over products' interests (see Chapter 4, "Information Flow Patterns Reveal Waste"). The silo view leads to work being accumulated between silos, stopping the product's transformation and generating the inventory and waiting types of waste. By its nature, the silo view leads to a lot of back and forth between silos, generating overprocessing, transportation and motion types of waste. The silo view or mentality is also behind pushing unfinished work or defects to the next silo, which can then translate into the defects type of waste. A particular case of pushing unfinished work is advancing the product transformation with open, not closed, *knowledge gaps*. In broader terms, a knowledge gap reflects what is not sufficiently known about a subject. Proceeding with open knowledge gaps guarantees rework much later in the product's transformations, with big schedule and cost impacts. For example, in Ted's story, one big knowledge gap was regarding the sizing case. As the FSAF team was facing pressure to run cases quickly because of the suppliers' employees being idle (see Appendix C1), work started and proceeded with the *fully operational case* as the sizing case, until the realization (almost 10 months later) that *the attachment case* is the real sizing case, forcing the reset of the approach and starting the design cycle all over again (see Appendix C3, Boom 3 icon). The push system and the attached silo view or mentality are fueling the Waste Machine.

5.3.2 Lack of Knowledge

As mentioned earlier, there are aggravating factors on top of the push system. One of them is the available knowledge or the lack thereof (see Figure 5.3–3). *Lack of knowledge* can manifest itself in various forms: using the wrong methodology, using the wrong formulas, using the wrong tools, using the good tools the wrong way, interpreting data the wrong way, omitting or ignoring important technical aspects or information, emphasizing not important technical aspects, searching for information in the wrong places, using the wrong references, etc., and in the end, leads to making mistakes. The most obvious type of waste generated by the lack of knowledge is *defects*. In a siloed organization, every individual silo has specific knowledge that is different from the other silos. This knowledge is typically mismanaged or lacks integration. Even within a silo, the knowledge level is not the same for all people. Typically, the top specialists have an extensive working knowledge, the entry-level specialists come out of universities and have little working knowledge. This situation creates an interesting phenomenon: the existence of silos within silos, corresponding to top specialists keeping their tacit knowledge acquired through the years for themselves and using it to consolidate their positions and acquire more power. Unfortunately, while working in silos, knowledge is put to work for the silo's interest, not for the product's interest. This comes out strongly in design reviews, where most of the specialists from each individual function hold their perspective as being the most important to consider and disregarding other perspectives that might be better suited for the product. A particular application of lack of knowledge is related to knowledge gaps. For example, in Ted's story, the design approach radically changed once the most senior "FSAF" specialist returned from sick leave (see Appendix

C4, Boom 4 icon), more than 10 months after work began. This means that the FSAF specialists initially working on the critical component couldn't even identify the knowledge gap surrounding the approach "frame and component" because of their lack of knowledge. Lack of knowledge makes it such that knowledge gaps cannot even be identified. Definitely, the lack of knowledge fuels the Waste Machine. For more about knowledge gaps, see *Success Is Assured.*[1]

5.3.3 Lack of Visibility and Office Politics

Another aggravating factor on top of a push system is the surrounding working environment, reflected by *lack of visibility* and *office politics* (see Figure 5.3–3). As we saw in Chapter 1, in the tangled environment, there's a blurred view of what the product or service is and who needs it, as well as how this product or service reaches the one who pays for it; there's very low visibility for stakeholders on the overall product or service transformation. In this environment, the holistic view of the process gets lost, with each stakeholder's individual view prevailing, becoming fertile ground for hidden agendas, internal competition, backstabbing, manipulation – or, in other words, office politics. The lack of visibility of a product's transformation generates mostly the *waiting* type of waste. In a siloed organization, every individual silo has their own objectives driving their priorities. This translates into poor inter-silo visibility and coordination regarding a product's transformation. This poor visibility translates into work that is done too soon by some or work that is done too late for others, with the net impact of delaying the product's transformation at best. Schedules, action plans and governance are the typical means to coordinate inter-silo work, but they can't make up for lack of visibility, especially when conditions change constantly, and everybody needs to be updated. For example, in Ted's story, the lack of visibility of a product's transformation translates into not knowing when the product will be finished. As you can see in Appendix C1, the first group of iterations, every next step is dependent on the current findings. If there's a fail, the team needs to meet, decide what lever to use and what values to choose for the lever, without knowing if the change is going to translate into a pass. If we separately ask MECH, STRU, THEL, DSGN, FSAF or CMGT representatives at what transformation stage the product is, the best we can get is blank stares. They might tell something about the tasks they'd accomplished or about the task at hand but little on the overall advancement. Maybe INTG could give an estimation.

Office politics generate mostly the *defects* type of waste. Let's consider the example in Chapter 3, where the manager, motivated by organizational politics (see Figure 3.6), pressures people to deliver regardless of the quality.

The short-term gain of delivering to plan, motivated by organizational politics, will be totally upset though by the rework required to be done later because of the non-quality. A more subtle and damaging effect of office politics is related to people frustration, disengagement and even burnout, situations that will make them prone to making errors or quitting the company in the best case or going on medical leave in the worst case. This goes beyond the waste discussion and is a clear violation of the fundamental right of returning healthy from work. Lack of visibility and office politics definitely fuel the Waste Machine.

5.4 How to Deal with the Waste Machine?

So, we've learned about what fuels the Waste Machine and found that it's fueled by the *push system* and its by-product the *silo view or mentality*, along with aggravating factors like *lack of knowledge, open knowledge gaps, lack of visibility* and *office politics*. Understanding this is going to be helpful in the next part dealing with how to remove waste.

Removing waste comes down to how to stop fueling the Waste Machine. With less and less fuel, the machine is less and less effective, slows down and generates less and less output (see Figure 5.4). So we need to find ways to increase visibility, to inhibit office politics, to timely close knowledge gaps, to use properly the right tools, to make sure there's knowledge, to inhibit the silo view This way, there's going to be fewer defects, less waiting, less inventory, less overprocessing, which in turn will bring costs and on-time-delivery under control.

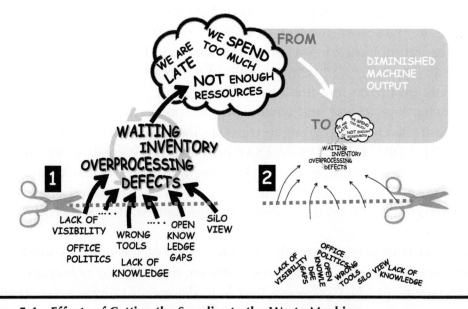

Figure 5.4   Effects of Cutting the Supplies to the Waste Machine.

5.4.1 The Flow System

All of this means that we must establish a new fundamental system to drive work.

As we saw, in the current setting, we have a push system, so we need something to replace it. Looking at alternatives that have been proven in practice to be profitable replacements, we will find the *flow system* (see Figure 5.5). By the way it works, the flow system is the opposite of a push system. *It is driven by the commitment and dedication to consistently give paying customers what they need, when they need it, safely, with quality and profitably – the least wasteful way.*

The main goal of a flow system is to enable the continuous transformation of the product or service since the demand for it until it gets in the hands of the paying customer when it is needed by the customer and without defects. This means that work is performed without interruptions or returns, according to what the transformation stage of the product requires and when it is required and means that decisions are always made in the best interest of the customer and, by extension, in the best interest of the product. The continuous transformation of the product drives less waiting, less inventory,

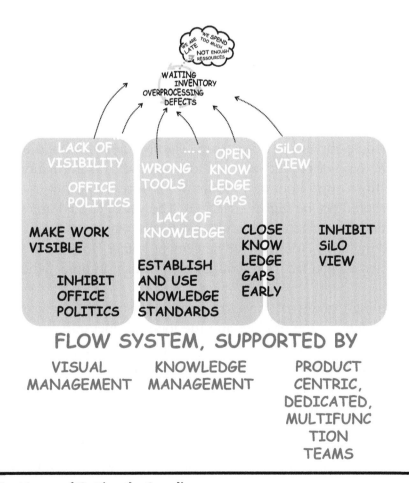

Figure 5.5   Means of Cutting the Supplies.

fewer defects – in other words less waste – ensuring the shortest lead times, the highest quality and the lowest costs.

The flow system in the case of a multifunction environment with multiple interdependencies where the product is hard to see and the work is not repetitive is supported by several fundamentals like *Visual Management, Knowledge Management, product-centric, dedicated, multifunction teams,* along with specific mechanisms like processing *one at a time* and the *flow regulator,* all backed by a relentless focus on the *customer's needs.*

5.4.2 Visual Management

Please note that Visual Management is a huge subject, we're just scratching the surface here.

Visual management is the practice of using information visualization techniques to manage work. This implies that all the elements required to manage work are captured, made visible, are easily accessible to the working team in a single place, usually a physical board. It is managed by the working team and facilitates decision-making and problem-solving as they are performing daily work, with the main objective of *being proactive.* Visual management covers several work aspects. Here are some examples, in no particular order: work to be done, work in execution, work finished, decisions, flow of activities in time, plan to actual, standardized work. The visual needs to show what happens in real time, be made such that the abnormal situation stands out without any interpretation and needs to have a set of a few simple rules to be able to operate it. The visual can be consulted or operated any time of day by individual contributors and/or during scheduled huddles by the working team. The frequency of huddles depends mainly on the type of product and the total product transformation time and could range from every hour to a minimum of once a day, but in order to be effective, it should not be higher than that. The visual should answer all the basic questions that someone unfamiliar with the work could ask: on what are you working now? How's the advancement going? How much is left to do? What problems do you face? Are you going to finish on time? Where do you need help?

There is a high variety of ways to set up the visual, which, again, is heavily dependent on the product and the total product transformation time: time-based setup, product transformation steps-based setup, workload-based setup. Let's take, for example, the *commitment-based schedule,* which is a time-based setup, and see how it looks (see Figure 5.6). It is mainly used in new product development work but could be applied to any project type of work.

The layout is simple, with columns and lines. The first line is reserved for the time line, the second for the main product transformation steps and the rest for each contributor-committed work (see Figure 5.6–1). The first column is

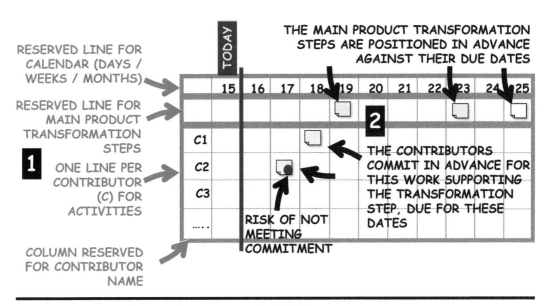

Figure 5.6   Example Commitment-Based Schedule.

reserved for the names of the contributors. The way it works is simple too (see Figure 5.6–2): the main product transformation steps are placed with sticky notes on the reserved line against the due date; each contributor commits to work supporting the transformation steps and places the corresponding sticky note on their reserved line. This all happens before the work starts when the team is in the planning stage. Work is managed through daily huddles, where all the contributors are present and give insights on how work advances. For example, let's say we're in the daily huddle, the 15th, and that C2 has problems and exposes the risk of not meeting the commitment for the 17th. Once this is exposed, both verbally and with a big red dot on the sticky note, the team looks to find ways to overcome the problems or, in the worst case, to escalate them. As you can see, this is a proactive way of dealing with issues, meeting the intent of visual management. Managing work with visual management helps to reduce significantly the waiting and defects types of waste. Visual management contributes to making work visible, inhibiting office politics by offering visibility to all, inhibiting silo view by bringing together the multifunction contributors around the product's needs (see Figure 5.5).

5.4.3 Knowledge Management

Please note that Knowledge Management is a huge subject, we're just scratching the surface here.

According to Wikipedia, Knowledge Management (KM) is the process of creating, sharing, using and managing the knowledge of an organization. It refers to a multidisciplinary approach to achieving organizational objectives by making the best use of knowledge.

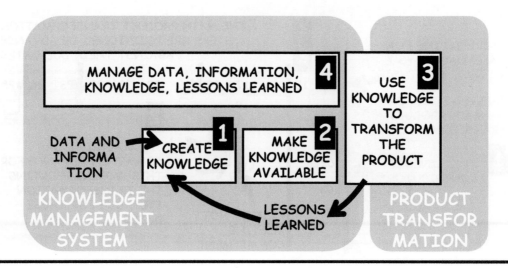

Figure 5.7   KM Basics.

KM systems are intrinsically linked with the transformation of the product. In order to have a continuous transformation of the product, the KM system needs to make available the required knowledge when required by the product transformation – in other words, it implies *having the right knowledge at the right moment when transforming the product.*

Figure 5.7 depicts the KM system basics and the link with product transformation. Here's a brief clarification of the terms. *Data* refers to raw numbers coming directly from calculations, tests or other measurements, while *information* refers to data that is processed by means of analysis or consolidation in a certain context – for example, in reports or memos. *Knowledge* refers to a collection and synthesis of information related to certain topics covering the product or to the transformation process. *Lessons learned* refers to the practice of collecting data and information while transforming the product and then using it to update existing knowledge or create new knowledge.

First, knowledge needs to be created from data and from information (see Figure 5.7–1); then, when used, it needs to be updated with lessons learned. Second, knowledge needs to be made available (see Figure 5.7–2) for use when the product transformation requires it. Third, benefits from using knowledge come once we use it, so knowledge usage needs to be mandated (see Figure 5.7–3) for a product's transformation. At the same time, knowledge is improved when used by the intermediary of lessons learned. The whole system relies on managing these basics, usually through an information technology platform (see Figure 5.7–4).

What is called broadly knowledge comes in various forms, from detailed checklists, user guides, to standards. Standards are mandatory references or instructions on how to perform work and are used during the product transformation or to prove compliance once the product is finished. In the new product development world, there are different types of standards: design standards that provide guidelines and methodologies on how to design, project and program standards that provide guidelines and methodologies on how to run a project or a program and the common theme is that they are pretty much the same from company to company. *Knowledge standards* are different; they provide references for decision-making, and they reflect the proprietary knowledge of the company because they are built around the company's products.

Their main characteristic is the graphical form where the known zone delimited by the existing company products and the unknown zone are clearly identified (see Figure 5.8), raising the awareness of possible knowledge gaps. Being in the red zone is not a bad thing; it's just an indication that we're in uncharted territory. So, knowledge standards help us to be proactive when a new product is developed. A knowledge standard would have been helpful in Ted's story: "Because of the severe conditions the component was exposed to (never encountered by our other products), the sizing case was not the 'fully operative case' but the 'attachment case.'" The never encountered before conditions would have been translated into a higher performance required by the new product and consequently into a dot in the unknown zone (see Figure 5.8–1). This would have automatically triggered an investigation around the sizing case. Unfortunately, work started and proceeded with the *fully operational case* as the sizing case until the realization (almost ten months later) that the *attachment case* is the real sizing case, forcing the reset of the approach and starting the design cycle all over again (see Appendix C3, Boom 3 icon). Using knowledge standards and a KM system helps to reduce significantly the defects type of waste. KM contributes to establishing and using knowledge standards, closing knowledge gaps early, making knowledge available, directing toward the use of the right tools (see Figure 5.5).

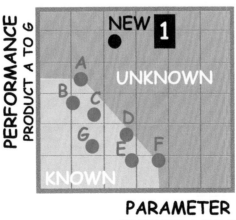

Figure 5.8   Generic Knowledge Standard.

5.4.4 Product-Centric, Dedicated Multifunction Teams

As their names show, these teams are *product-oriented*, which means it is *the required transformation of the product that dictates the selection of team members*. It is multifunction because in tangled environments, the norm is that several functions contribute to the transformation. Instead of working in their respective silos and passing work between silos while having to resolve conflicting priorities, the members are now in an environment where they have a common team objective and shared responsibility for delivering the product. Ownership is obvious now. Hidden agendas, internal competition, backstabbing, manipulation have less fertile ground in this environment.

They are *dedicated* full time to transforming and delivering the product. The outcome of being involved with more than one product at a time is an increased risk of not delivering on time (see Figure 5.9).

In Figure 5.9–1, we can see the effect of working on three projects at the same time, jumping from one to another to meet the schedule for each. Besides the high risk of delivering all three of them late, there's the additional risk of creating more defects, as we lose continuity in the process of jumping from one to another. Losing continuity calls for additional adjustments to see where we left off and what needs to be done next, adding more time to the time line. As we can easily see in Ted's example in Chapter 3, it is obvious that the resources were split between different projects. If we look now at Figure 5.9–2 and use the same workload, the risk of not delivering any of the three projects on time is much less for fully dedicated resources. Additionally, on the important topic of

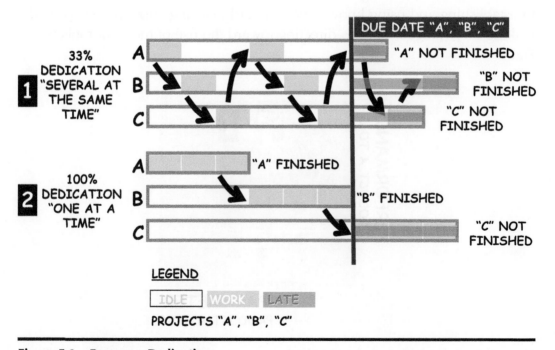

Figure 5.9   Resource Dedication.

employee engagement, people are less frustrated; they have a feeling of accomplishment that increases their engagement. In the first case though, they are less engaged because of the frustration of not being able to deliver: "Look, we missed delivering all three projects." Working with product-centric, dedicated multifunction teams contributes to inhibiting the siloed view, to inhibiting office politics and to facilitating making work visible, with the additional benefit of increasing employee engagement.

A word of caution about the ever-present SWAT or Tiger Teams (names can vary), very popular in the tangled environment. They are not to be confounded with the product-centric multifunctional teams we've described in this chapter. Although they are multidisciplinary, their scope of work and operational mode are different. SWAT or Tiger Teams are formed once a big issue appears, and they are dismantled as the issue gets under control. They work relentlessly to regain control, disrupting other operations if the situation requires it. Usually, this represents a big effort to put a patch in place, as they rarely address the underlying root causes behind the issue.

5.4.5 Dealing with Behavioral and Cultural Aspects

Working in the tangled environment is tedious because the holistic view of the process gets lost, with each stakeholder's individual view prevailing, resulting in conflicting interests that are hard to resolve. Office politics aggravate these conflicts. The career paths, the bonuses and the individual aspirations of the ones involved are tied to the silo's objectives, which in most cases are not aligned. This becomes fertile ground for distorting, misdirecting, suppressing or withholding information to serve self-interests. Cultural patterns, like a decision by a committee or micromanagement, are direct by-products of this.

There's no silver bullet in trying to address behavioral and cultural aspects. Having said that, let's consider how dedicated multifunction teams and visual management can inhibit the behavior described in Chapter 3, with the manager motivated by organizational politics (see Figure 3.6) who pressures people to deliver regardless of the quality. In the first two situations, (see Figure 3.6–1, 2) the main motivation comes from a "divide and conquer" strategy and from internal competition. Using product-centric, dedicated, multifunction teams, these situations are less likely to happen because we're not in a silo setting anymore. It's not a competition between functions anymore and achieving functions' goals is not relevant anymore. The third situation is different though (see Figure 3.6–3) and can happen even in the multifunction team environment. This is where visual management comes into play. With the visibility provided for the required work to be performed, skipping steps will appear as an abnormality easily identifiable on the visual, which will make it harder to be hidden or ignored.

Table 5.2 summarizes some alternatives to dealing with information flow patterns (see Figure 4.3), which include cultural aspects.

Table 5.2 Ways of Dealing with Information Flow Patterns

INFO PATTERN	ASPECT	WASTE GENERATED	WAYS TO DEAL WITH IT
People to people	Micromanagement, Office Politics	Defects, Overprocessing and Waiting	Visual Management, Dedicated Multifunction Teams
Meeting to meeting	Excessive Governance, Decision by Committee	Waiting and Overprocessing	Visual Management, Dedicated Multifunction Teams
Inbox to inbox	Excessive Emailing, Silos	Waiting, Overprocessing and Overproduction	Visual Management, Dedicated Multifunction Teams, KM
Automated workflow	Tool Dependence, Silos	Waiting	Visual Management, Dedicated Multifunction Teams, KM

The following sections are particularly of interest for the VSM facilitators.

5.5 What's the Future State Strategy?

Now that we understand how the Waste Machine works and have seen some ways of dealing with it, we're at a point where the direction in which to design the future state starts to be clearer. In order to crystalize our thoughts, we need to position all the future state considerations in a schematic called the *future state strategy*. The future state strategy is done having in mind the future state criteria, the means to deal with waste and the technical backbone (Figure 5.1–1 to 4).

How is it done? *Linking the essential activities from the technical backbone in a way to have less waste and to enable flow to set up for meeting the objectives.* We already saw how visual management, product-centric, dedicated, multifunction teams and KM help achieve this, but as mentioned earlier, there are additional means to be considered, among which we can mention the following:

- Single entry point: the only point in the process where the tasks to manage work or the products to be processed are collected and available for everybody to see.
- Flow regulator: a controlled point that dictates the flow rate to the rest of the process; this could be one (recommended) or several in the case where full continuity cannot be achieved (see the icon in Appendix B).

- Supermarket: regulates the consumer – supplying activities and works on the principle "take one, put one back" – processing information one at a time, so as we consume one piece of information, the one supplying needs to make available other required information; this ensures seamless processing and making sure the information is not generated too early, with the risk of becoming out-of-date (see the icon in Appendix B).
- First in first out: regulates the consumer – supplying activities with the goal of processing information one at a time in the arrival order and with a finite backlog in the pipeline; this ensures seamless processing, with a controlled inventory of information in between (see the icon in Appendix B).
- Single information repository: the only place where the generated information related to the transformation of the product or other information required to perform work is stored.

Another aspect to be considered while building the future state strategy is the implementation time line. Designing a future state that will take more than six months to implement is risky because in the tangled environment, the more time passes by, the less the focus and dedication to execute the required changes. Don't forget, old habits prevail! *The future state needs to have the right mix of meaningful changes to depart from the current state and an implementation time line ensuring a fast transition.* This is a critical consideration.

Let's hear Ted's explanations of the rationale of building the future state strategy for the critical component requirements to the supplier (Ted's story).

Our future state criteria (see Appendix E1) clearly set the path to lead time reduction through less reliance on emails, meetings and chasing to advance work, with all stakeholders having aligned priorities, having less errors, having real-time visibility on the overall advancement, having a proactive start of the process. We kept it handy while we were designing the future state.

We started by making fundamental changes in the technical backbone (see Appendix E2) to make sure the process will flow better. By design, the old technical backbone was based on a lot of back and forth due to the iterations. Although they are not waste, iterations have the downside of not knowing in advance when an answer will be found, thus working with a virtually infinite time line. It is not uncommon to hear in our environment, "We don't know if we're going to have an answer, let alone when we'll have it …" In the new technical backbone, this is countered by using design of experiments. According to Wikipedia, Design of experiments (DOE) is defined as a branch of applied statistics that deals with planning, conducting, analyzing and interpreting controlled tests to evaluate the factors that control the value of a parameter or group of parameters. The advantage of using DOE is you know in advance how many runs you need to perform, making it easier to schedule because you know how much work is required for a run. The other advantage of using DOE is you're using it to close knowledge gaps related to the lever values for safe component operation in a structured fashion. The lever is an input parameter that can be dialed up or down with the purpose of improving the output. Once the knowledge gaps are closed by performing the runs, we can rely on the regression coming from the DOE analysis to start converging toward the best options by making trade-offs, which then becomes the basis for setting the requirements. Now, you cannot just jump into a DOE without closing some basic knowledge gaps. In our case, they were relative to the required performance for the product, the required cases, the assumptions, the levers and their values, the compatibility of models ... all the things that triggered the errors we made. So, we divided the new technical backbone into three essential activities and included them in the future state strategy: (1) Closing basic knowledge gaps. (2) Experiment. (3) Converge and decide [see Figure 5.10–1].

With this, we've addressed having a proactive start of the process and having less errors, from the future state criteria.

Then, we've decided to use FIFOs [see Figure 5.10–6] for running the experiments and the convergence, and this is how we ended up with two flow regulators [see Figure 5.10–5]. For us, it was not possible to have just one flow regulator because we couldn't start the convergence before knowing the DOE results. The implication is that the process is now split, and there's an accumulation of information sitting between the two. This didn't really bother us because it's a good trade for getting out of the back and forth and being more predictable in terms of lead time.

To reduce reliance on emails, meetings and chasing to advance work and to make sure we have aligned priorities and adequate visibility of work for all stakeholders, we decided to add in the future state strategy the product-centric, dedicated, multifunction team [see Figure 5.10–2] using visual management

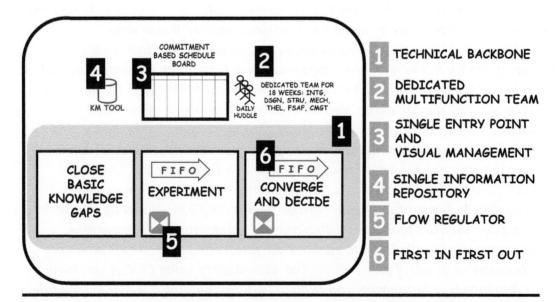

Figure 5.10   Future State Strategy for the Critical Component Requirements to Supplier.

[see Figure 5.10–3] and a single information repository [see Figure 5.10–4]. In this setting, the commitment-based schedule board [see Figure 5.6] becomes the single-entry point for all tasks [see Figure 5.10–3].

As you can see, to ensure a fast implementation, we considered more rearranging of the way we work rather than costly information system changes, which we all know require a lot of time. Our drive while building the strategy was "brain before wallet," working more intelligently before spending more money. ... Something related to this – we were not at the first attempt to use DOE in new product development, but until now, it was always seen as a "nice to have" practice because of the perception that "it takes too long." This time around, we had a clear case of how long it takes and how much it costs when we're not using it [smiling].

5.6 Mapping the Future State

The future state strategy is the basis for building the future state map. As we saw in Chapter 3, there are several levels of granularity when mapping. As a general rule, map the future state at the same level of granularity as the current state to have a fair comparison basis. Because of the way they build on each other, the recommended way to proceed is the following: derive the high-level future state map from the future state strategy (see Figure 5.1–5) and then from it derive the detailed future state map.

5.6.1 Time to Practice

Based on Figure 5.10 and the related information provided by Ted, please draw the high-level future state map using icons from Appendix B and answer the following questions:

- What icons did you use in the high-level future state map? How did you position them?
- What was the rationale behind your choices?

5.6.2 High-Level Future State Map

Here's what Ted has to say about how the team designed the high-level future state map (Ted's story):

Once we had the future state strategy sorted out, we looked at the high-level current state map [see Figure 3.19] because we wanted to map the future state at the same level. We used the same instructions on how to do it, kept the activities at a fairly high level in the order set by the future state strategy and inserted key information flow and time line elements [see Figure 5.11].

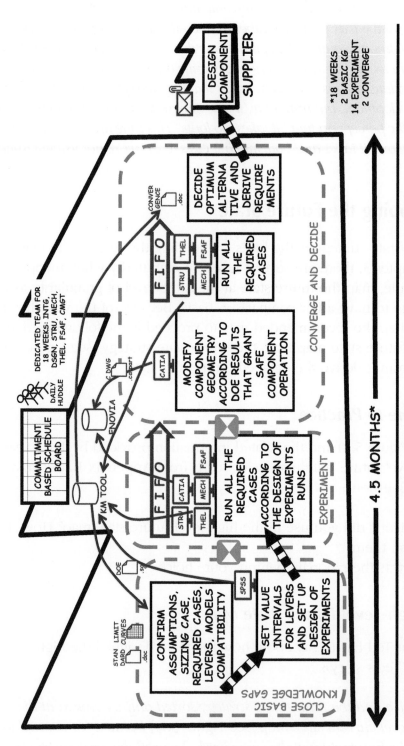

Figure 5.11 High-Level Future State VSM for the Critical Component Requirements to Supplier.

We considered six high-level activities reflecting well the three elements of the technical backbone, and we linked them in the map with the push arrows and the FIFOs to show how the transformation of the component requirements occurs. [smiling] Yes, there's push in the future state, and we didn't fall for a utopic "flow it all the way," considering the business we're in and the type of work we perform – we aimed for something more realistic and feasible. We added the big information flow items corresponding to the activities, more precisely: the models we use, the statistical analysis software, the standards and the limit curves, the KM tool as the single information repository, the FIFOs and the new documents for DOE and convergence. We didn't forget about Outlook, but we wanted to represent the fact that in the future state, Outlook is not a key player anymore, even if we will probably continue to use it sporadically. We didn't forget about the schedule either, but we didn't include the schedule icon, just to represent the fact that we were relying on the visual board to manage the tasks according to the big milestones – no more need for detailed schedules. Then we added the two flow regulators next to the high-level activities that will drive flow in the new process.

As you can see, there's no more seven internal entities involved anymore, but just one. This reflects the fact that we want to operate as a dedicated multidisciplinary team. To enhance this, we added the commitment-based board, the daily huddles, the functions represented in the team and the duration the team will work together. We draw the dotted blue boxes to highlight that all the activities contained within them are managed by the visual board.

In the end, we estimated the total time line by considering realistic times that the three essential activities could take: 2 weeks for closing the basic knowledge gaps, 14 weeks for experimenting, 2 weeks for converging, for a total of 18 weeks or 4.5 months. We estimated 14 weeks for experimenting based on the same number of levers we used in the current state, considering a 32-run DOE and a workload of 2 days per run.

While mapping, we kept an eye on the future state strategy and made sure all the elements recorded there were placed in the high-level future state map.

What I noticed during the future state workshop was how much the team dynamic changed from the beginning. We started in a rather uncooperative mood where people would refrain from talking to each other, to excitement as their understanding about the problems and the solutions grew. This continued as we started to map the detailed future state.

5.6.3 Detailed-Level Future State Map

*We used the high-level future state map [see Figure 5.11] and the A-B-C
sequence with the mapping pattern [see Figure 3.2] to show how we want to
work in the future in more detail. To do that, we took the high-level elements
one at a time and mapped in more detail for each of them, adding the
information flow required to perform them [see Figure 5.12–1 to 4].*

*While mapping, we looked at the level of granularity of the detailed current
state to make sure we have a fair comparison. For the activities flow for "close
basic knowledge gaps" [see Figure 5.12–1], we derived five activities from the
two in the high level, and we added the kick-off activity at the beginning.
We linked the activities with push arrows because they are building on each
other and respected the precedence between them. So basically, we start with
revising the required product performance, making sure we understand
what's new from previously developed products. At the same time, we
determine and clarify the component's performance and the drivers; then we
decide what cases need to be run to ensure safe operation. Once we do all of
this, we're setting the initial geometry, and we ensure that the models we use
are compatible. This last activity is critical and the one that takes most of the
two weeks we're planning for this stage because it includes all the necessary
corrections and adjustments – remember how much trouble this caused us?
After that, we decide the levers and the value intervals for each of them and
set up the DOE. We used the people icon with all the team functions listed
below to illustrate that the respective activities are performed together as a
team.*

*Then, we completed the information flow to show what documents and
models are used, where we have manipulation of information, where we need
to check [smiling]. As you can see, there are still emails going on. Important
to notice, there are new documents to be used: standards, limit curves, basic
knowledge gaps and DOE, which are all linked with the new knowledge
management tool we will use as the single information repository [see
Figure 5.13]. The new model we didn't use before is SPSS, a statistical analysis
software, which helps with setting and analyzing the DOE.*

*The activities flow for "Experiment" went from one activity in the high level
to six [see Figure 5.12–2]. You might recognize the first five activities from the
detailed current state map; they remain basically the same, with the notable
mention they are now performed in a preestablished sequence given by the
DOE set up, at the end of "Closing basic knowledge gaps" [see Figure 5.12–1].
At the end of each DOE run, the results are recorded. They will feed the last
activity, the DOE analysis. As you can see, there's no push arrows anymore
between activities, the reason being we now follow the FIFO generated by
the DOE set up. No more throw it over the fence or going back. … To make
this point obvious, we inserted the flow regulator icon next to providing the
geometry activity. The people icon shows what activities are done by each*

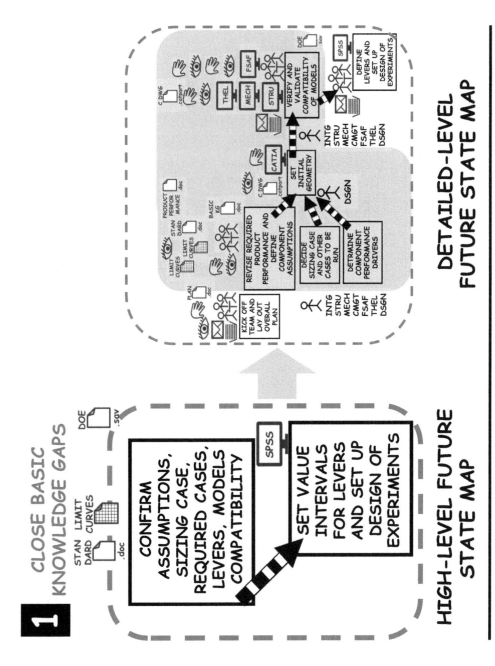

Figure 5.12   1: Detailing the Future State VSM for the Critical Component Requirements to Supplier – Close Basic Knowledge Gaps. (*Continued*)

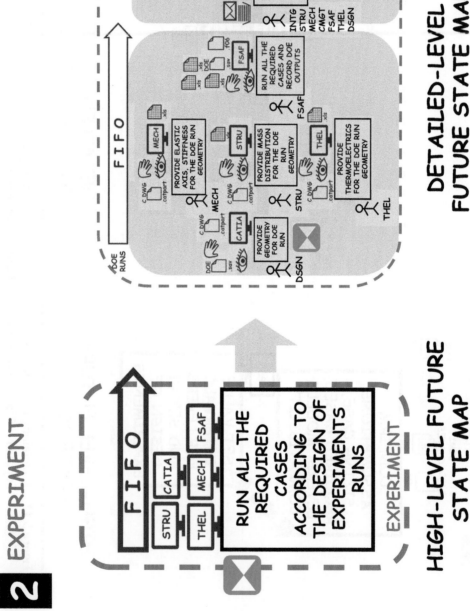

Figure 5.12 (*Continued*) 2: Detailing the Future State VSM for the Critical Component Requirements to Supplier – Experiment. (*Continued*)

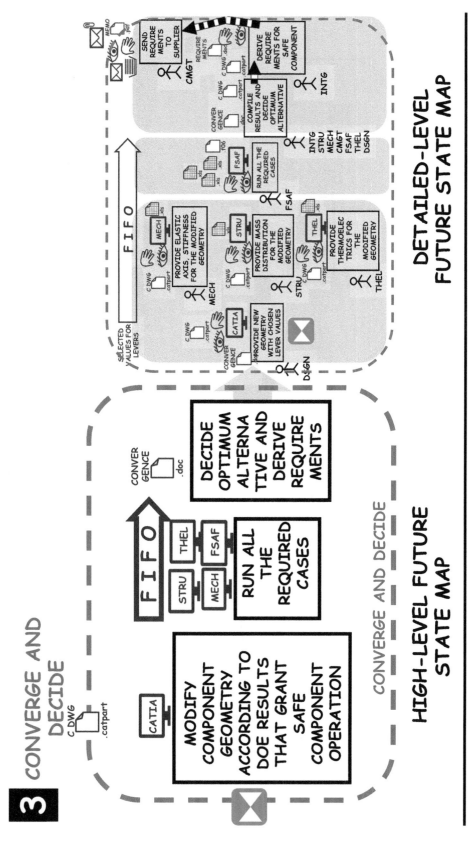

Figure 5.12 (*Continued*) 3: Detailing the Future State VSM for the Critical Component Requirements to Supplier – Coverage and Decide. (*Continued*)

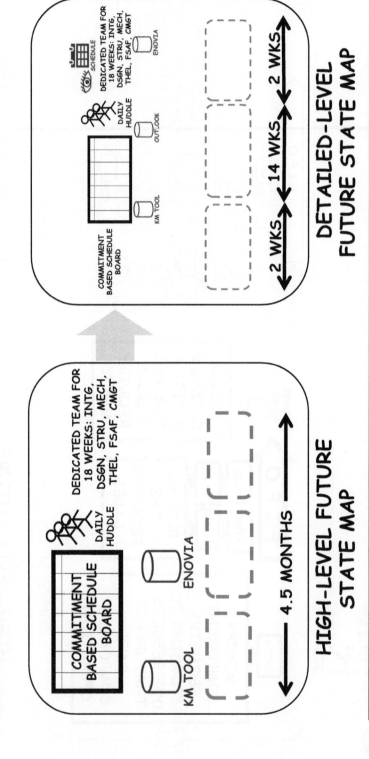

4 DATABASES, VISUAL MANAGEMENT, TIME LINE

COMMITMENT BASED SCHEDULE BOARD

DAILY HUDDLE

DEDICATED TEAM FOR 18 WEEKS: INTG, DSGN, STRU, MECH, THEL, FSAF, CMGT

KM TOOL

ENOVIA

4.5 MONTHS

HIGH-LEVEL FUTURE STATE MAP

COMMITMENT BASED SCHEDULE BOARD

DAILY HUDDLE

SCHEDULE

DEDICATED TEAM FOR 18 WEEKS: INTG, DSGN, STRU, MECH, THEL, FSAF, CMGT

KM TOOL

OUTLOOK

ENOVIA

2 WKS   14 WKS   2 WKS

DETAILED-LEVEL FUTURE STATE MAP

Figure 5.12 (*Continued*) 4: Detailing the Future State VSM for the Critical Component Requirements to Supplier – Databases, visual management, time line.

function individually and as a group, similar to "Closing basic knowledge gaps."

The information flow icons are not new either. They include our models, the output files from the models, the checking and manipulation of information, the drawing. What's new is the DOE document that contains the order of runs, which is the starting point for the FIFO, then is used to compile the individual results from the runs at the end of the FIFO and then is used to analyze the DOE once all the runs are finished. We used the same icon SPSS software for doing the DOE analysis. As mentioned earlier, the FIFO is generated by the DOE setup, starts from providing the geometry and ends at the recording of results. The way it works is the setup dictates the geometries which will be used to provide the FSAF analysis the needed inputs. We estimated 32 DOE runs by keeping the same five levers as in the current state, so there's going to be a maximum of 32 FSAF analyses in the FIFO pipeline. The difference is this time is not about "does it pass or does it fail" anymore … it is about learning as much as possible on what the variation in the levers values does to the safety of the component.

The activities flow for "converge and decide" went from three in the high level to eight [see Figure 5.12–3]. Similarly to "Experiment," you can see the same activities related to the analysis, but for different cases this time around. They are followed by the compilation of results and the decision, which then becomes the basis for deriving the requirements and sending them to the supplier [smiling]. Yes, the push arrows are back, this time from deciding the optimum alternative until sending the requirements to the supplier. We used the same rationale as in "Experiment" for not inserting push arrows for the previous activities, the only difference being that now is the analysis of the DOE that will dictate the values and the order in which the new cases are run. The same for the flow regulator icon next to providing geometry activity. Running the new cases will take most of the estimated two weeks total time line for "converge and decide." What is important to realize is that the DOE explores the whole range of possibilities of using the levers, so the other cases needed to be run will not be in a position where we might expect fail results but rather confirm the safety of the component – we estimated a maximum of five runs; this is why the time line is so short. The people icon shows what activities are done by each function individually and as a group, like in "Experiment" and "Closing basic knowledge gaps."

The first new icon in the information flow is the convergence document which is derived from the DOE document, used at the beginning of the FIFO and used to compile the results at the end of the FIFO. The second new icon is the requirements document that is sent to the supplier. At the top of the information flow, there's the FIFO, starting from providing the geometry and generated by the convergence document, ending with the compilation of results.

Just a few things remained to complete the detailed future state map: the tools, the visual management, the information paths and the time line.

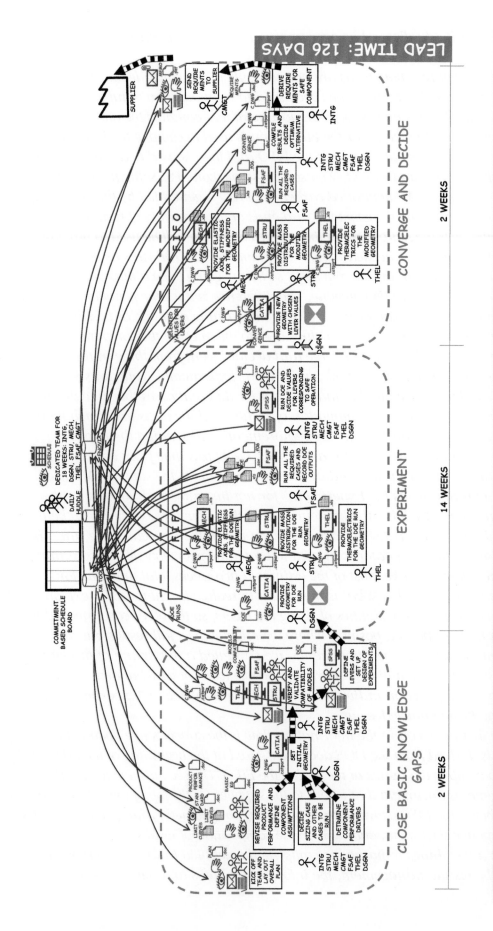

Figure 5.13 Detailed-Level Future State VSM for the Critical Component Requirements to Supplier.

We placed the KM tool, ENOVIA, and Outlook above the other information flow icons, and we added the schedule and check icons to illustrate that we use the schedule when managing the tasks on the visual board [see Figure 5.12–4].

Then we placed the visual board icon above, with the daily huddle, to show how we operate, with the entire team being present when discussing daily tasks. We drew the blue dotted line boxes around the activities that we manage through the visual board. We added the time line for each of the three essential activities, with the estimated total lead time in calendar days because that's how we recorded it in the current state. Finally, we drew all the information paths between the tools and documents, making sure we point the arrows in the right direction.

We added the time line at the bottom according to the estimated time intervals discussed at the high-level future state, then added the total lead time after we translated the 18 weeks in calendar days to match the current state lead time evaluation, which was in calendar days.

That was it; we finished drawing the detailed future state map! [You can see the mapping result in Figure 5.13.]. I can't express the feeling that we all had when we stepped back and looked at the map: relief, tiredness, joy and optimism would sum it up.

One can see the new orientation we were taking just by looking at the map. Now the process flows from left to right without returns and with less push. The big majority of the information path is linked with the new KM tool, and although we still have emails, one can see Outlook is not the main communication vehicle anymore. There's no more chasing, the daily huddles of the dedicated multifunction team and the commitment-based schedule board took care of it [smiling]. This is an absolute improvement over what we lived in the current state.

Most importantly, we can recognize this as a generic pattern of developing the requirements for our suppliers or even developing the new product itself, easily applicable in future development programs.

Note

1   Cloft, P. W., Kennedy, M. N., Kennedy, B. M. (2018). *Success is assured: Satisfy your customers on time and on budget by optimizing decisions collaboratively using reusable visual models.* ISBN-13: 978-1138618589, ISBN-10: 1138618586.

Chapter 6

Is It Good Enough? What Does It Take to Make It Work?

We are now at the point where the team understands the way out from the current situation, and even if the new notions related to the future state are not fully mastered, the team clearly sees how this might work. An important question needs to be answered though: is this future state going to make a difference? The answer is going to come from several exercises: simulating the future state, from looking at the *before and after* situations and by *rating against the future state criteria*. A nonsatisfactory answer to the question triggers a return to the future state design.

6.1 Simulating the Future State

The future state simulation is a necessary exercise that will answer the question: is this future state going to work better than the current state?

We usually do this by simulating on the future state map how things are going to work differently than in the current state. The simulation can be done in several ways, like following a current product through the stages and seeing the differences or by looking at current issues and seeing how they are avoided in the future state.

Let's see how Ted and his team went about it.

We all thought we're finished once the detailed future state was on the wall, but the facilitator brought us back to reality: there were some unanswered questions lingering, one of them being, "Is this going to make a difference?" So, we pulled out the cause and adverse effect table (see Appendix D2) and stick it next to the detailed future state map. Then we took each item from the table and asked the question: is this going to be caught by the future state? For instance, we took the visible cause 1 "Use of the FSAF model without being reconciled with the MECH model. Meshing mismatch" and started to walk the detailed future state [see Figure 6.1] to see what activity would catch it.

DOI: 10.4324/9781003050377-6

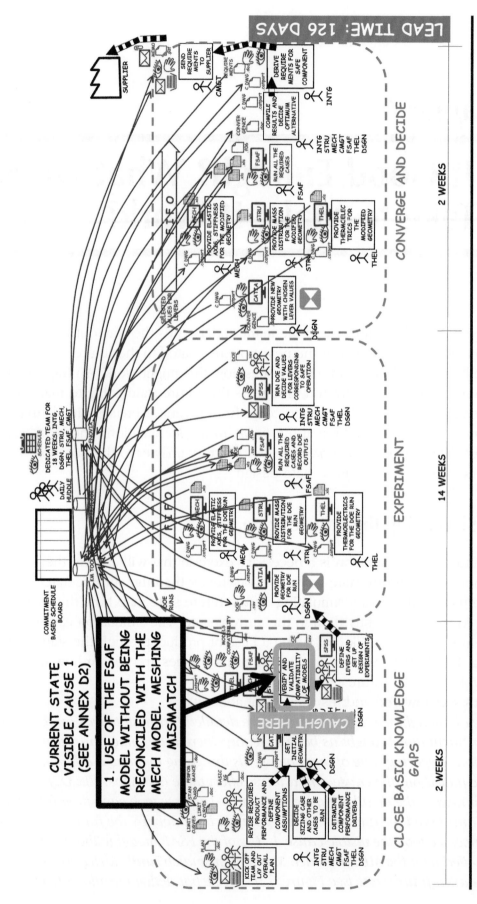

Figure 6.1 Detailed-Level Future State VSM Verification for the Critical Component Requirements to Supplier.

And sure enough, right at the beginning of the process, in the "Closing basic knowledge gaps," there's the "Verify and validate compatibility of models" activity that if performed early enough in the past would have made the mismatch visible and forced the required corrections before running the models. We added a sheet of paper next to the table and wrote our conclusion next to the visible cause 1. Then, we looked at all eight of them and did the same thing, recording the conclusions in the table [see Appendix F1]. In the end, we were reassured to see that they are all addressed in our future state and became even more convinced about being on the right path.

6.2 The Before and After

Comparing the before and after helps answer the question, How much better is the future state versus the current state? This brings another aspect than the future state simulation by putting the current and future maps next to each other and quantifying the changes to show the benefits. One thing to keep in mind is this should not become a chasing the numbers exercise; this should be done to illustrate the difference with orders of magnitude, not with decimals.

Let's hear how Ted and his team went about it.

We started the before and after by looking at the high-level value stream maps for the current and for the future state, then we compared them (see Figure 6.2). The first observation was the time line: from 15 months to 4.5 months. This allowed us to estimate an approximate 70% reduction. Even if we look at the initial planned time line of 10 months this represents approximately 50% reduction. The next observation was about the push arrows. First, the total count: we went from 10 to 3, an approximate 70% reduction in push arrows. Second, the returns: we had two return arrows, compared with 0, meaning 100% reduction in returns in the process – what was important though is we could explain clearly why there will be no returns in the future (see Figure 5.12–3 and explanations).

Once this exercise finished, we gathered in front of the detailed future state map (see Figure 5.13) and counted the icons, the same way as we did for the detailed current state map (see Appendix D1). As we were counting, we wrote the future state count next to the one in the current state (see Appendix F2). This gave us an indication of how much waste was removed. As an example, the current state had a total of 466 icons related to emails, meetings and chasing, while the future state had nine icons. Again, this is about order of magnitude, not decimals, so this means approximately 95% reduction. Other significant changes were recorded for: databases 70% reduction, files 90% reduction. We compiled all these observations into a summary table (see Figure 6.3) and used it to show the benefits.

Although this evaluation is not an exact science, it allowed us to somehow quantify and communicate the amount of waste we were taking out of the process and to confirm the future state as being much better than the current state.

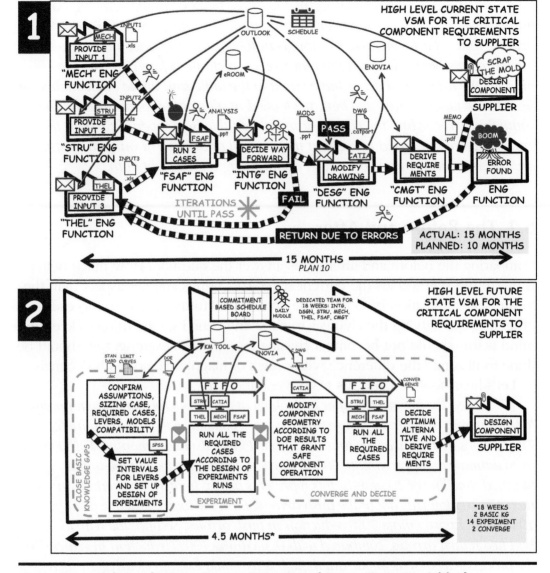

Figure 6.2   High Level VSM – Current State (1) and Future State (2), Critical Component Requirements to Supplier.

	Before	*After*	*Improvement*
TIME LINE MONTHS	15	4.5	70%
PUSH	10	3	70%
RETURNS	2	0	100%
EMAILS, MEETINGS, CHASERS	466	9	95%
DATABASES	10	3	70%
FILES	333	40	90%

Figure 6.3   Summary Before and After, Critical Component Requirements to Supplier.

6.3 Rating against the Future State Criteria

Rating against the future state criteria answers the question: did we consider the future state criteria when we designed the future state? There's a direct relationship between the current state conclusions and the future state criteria. The latter is derived from the former, ensuring that we are focused on the right things when designing the future state. This verification step is a sanity check, to make sure nothing deemed important was left out.

Let's hear how Ted and his team went about it.

Once completing the before-after summary table, we tackled the last verification point. We started another table [see Figure 6.4]. We wrote the first item from the future state criteria "Less than 221 days to release mature component requirements" [see Appendix E1] in the first column, then asked the first question: "How do we know the future state achieves this?" As a reminder, the less than 221 days comes from the mandate to cut the lead time in half (current was 442 days). We wrote the answer in the second column "126 days, see new time line calculation," translating the projected 18 weeks in calendar days to have a fair comparison with the current time line measured in calendar days. Then we asked the second question: "Did we fully or partially achieve this?" And we took a simple convention with a circle divided in four to represent various percentages of achievement: not achieved 0% empty circle, partially achieved from 25% with a blacked-out quarter circle to 75% with three blacked-out quarters, fully achieved 100% with the entire circle blacked out. Again, nothing scientific, just to have an order of

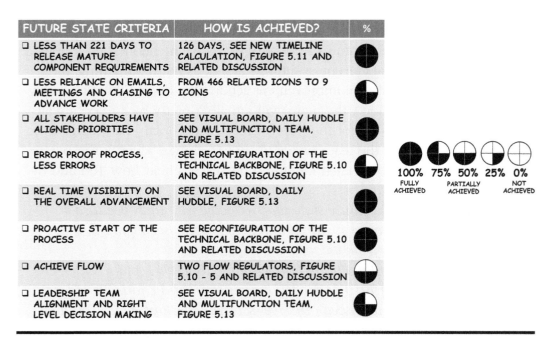

Figure 6.4   Future State VSM Rating against the Future State Criteria, Critical Component Requirements to Supplier.

magnitude. In this case, because of the 126 days being less than 221 days, we gave it a full blacked-out circle for 100% achievement. Then we continued evaluating the other items from the future state criteria, one after the other, and completed the table.

As you can see, we considered full achievement for four criteria, 75% partial achievement for three criteria and 50% partial achievement for "achieving flow" criteria.

What is important to mention is the good job the facilitator did to keep us honest, as we all tend to over evaluate our work, by asking questions related to why we thought the rating is good. This forced us to go back into explaining how the future state we designed works, contributing to elevate even more our level of understanding and the confidence level we had the right solutions.

Although it is not the case in Ted's story, it might happen to not meet some criteria. What to do then? First, consider this as an improvement opportunity, not as a failure. Remember, the team is still in learning mode, and it's just natural to oversee things. The verification stage did its job and caught it before the improvement plan is elaborated and executed. In this case, with the help of the facilitator, the team needs to go back to understand where the criteria came from. Once the team understands and is convinced the criteria is pertinent to improving the current state, then they need to make adjustments in the future state design to satisfy it.

6.4 The Future State Map Bursts

The bursts are highlights on the high-level or detailed-level future state map used to show what elements need to be implemented such that the map becomes a reality (see the icon in Appendix B). As we mentioned in Chapter 1, a value stream map, be it current or future state, does not fix anything; the execution of the value stream improvement action plan does. Without actually changing how work is done, the maps will remain a pretty picture on a wall.

The bursts are the basis for the improvement action plan that needs to be executed. At this stage, the team needs to do two things: identify the bursts and then give details about each identified burst. Let's hear how Ted and his team went about bursts:

We used the high-level future state map to locate the bursts because it captures well all the changes required to fix the process [see Figure 6.5]. So, we started methodically from the top:

Burst A: the dedicated multifunction team for 18 weeks, comprising INTG, DSGN, STRU, MECH, THEL, FSAF, CMGT engineering functions. In order to better understand this, we asked ourselves several questions: who should be the team members? What's going to be the reporting structure, and who needs to approve it? Who manages the team? Do we collocate the team members? If

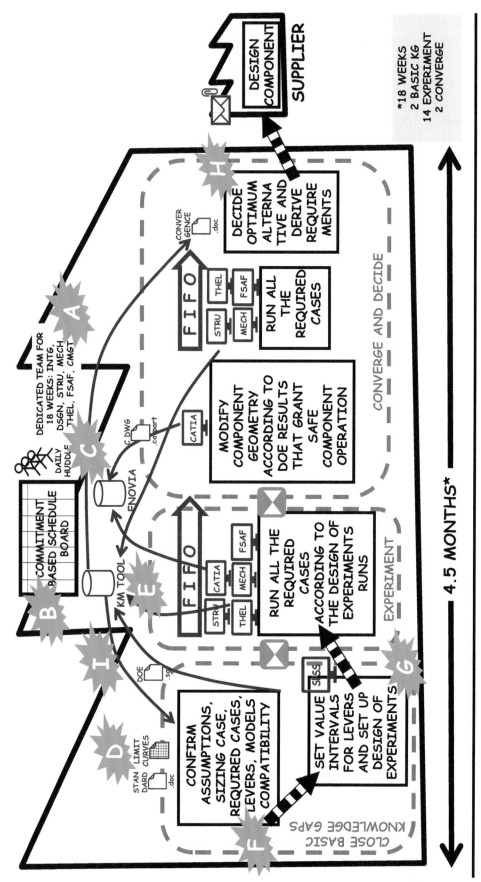

Figure 6.5   Bursts for the High-Level Future State VSM for the Critical Component Requirements to Supplier.

yes, what's the best place in the building, and who manages the move? After discussions, we listed in the burst details:

- *the names of the team members, largely being the ones involved in the value stream mapping exercise*
- *a matrix organizational structure where team members will report to the function manager and to the team leader*
- *my name as the team leader because the INTG function that I represent was already doing the coordination work*
- *to keep the same places for now, as the logistics of the move potentially being costly*
- *the new product development VPs name as the approver of the organizational changes we were proposing*

Burst B: the commitment-based schedule board. On this item, the discussions went around: where to install the board? Who designs it, and who hangs it on the wall? Then we started listing the proposal:

- *the conference room that we thought is convenient for all, and we knew is not occupied; as an additional advantage, we can use it for team meetings without having to make conference rooms reservations*
- *the name of the INTG team member as the one responsible to design and install the board*
- *the new product development VPs name as the approver of the room being dedicated to the team*

Burst C: the daily huddles. So, we answered some questions: where are they going to take place? What time of the day? For how long? Who leads the huddle? What's the objective of the daily huddle? What are the rules for the daily huddle? Do we need a computer to support discussions? Then we listed the proposal:

- *next to the commitment-based board in the proposed conference room*
- *start at 8:00 am for 30 min*
- *the name of the INTG team member to lead the daily huddle*
- *my name to set the objectives and the huddle rules*
- *the request to have a permanent projector in the conference room*

Burst D: standards, knowledge standards. Our starting questions went around: what are the critical ones we need to have as soon as possible? Who's going to document them? For when are they required? Where are they going to be located? What others are required? And then we realized there's not going to be any detailed recommendation for now; we need a workshop to answer all these questions, so we listed:

■ *need a workshop to establish a list of required standards, knowledge standards and the plan to document them – with my name next to it*

Burst E: the knowledge management tool. For this one, we knew we needed our IT friends to be involved, so we listed:

■ *find a temporary solution, more robust than our current eRooms – with my name next to it*

■ *work with IT and establish KM tool requirements, find software packages that fit our requirements and install the one that is the most suitable for us. This one was on me too [smiling]*

Burst F: the process for compatibility of models:

■ *workshop to set instructions on how to verify if the models are compatible or not, including decision criteria to identify when and what corrections are necessary – the multifunction team*

■ *revise our meshing standard if necessary – the name of the standard owner*

Burst G: the DOE process and document:

■ *instructions on how to set up the DOE and how the DOE document looks, including instructions on how to interpret the results and how to draw conclusions based on the results – the name of the INTG senior specialist*

Burst H: the convergence process and document:

■ *instructions on how the convergence is done and how the document looks, including decision criteria for finding the optimum alternative – the name of the INTG senior specialist*

Burst I: company-wide knowledge management system. This burst is more special. As we were discussing about the bursts D to H, we came to the realization that we need something at the company level to make sure we have a more structured approach to managing knowledge. We felt this will benefit the company in a significant way because what happened in the critical component requirements to the supplier was not an isolated case. At the same time, we realized this requires great attention from the company's leadership team and decided to mention it in our recommendations, just to bring attention to the higher-ups and not necessarily as an item for us to manage. We thought implementation of D to H is enough to ensure achievement of the objectives for the future state, so we recommended:

> ■ *make awareness on establishing a company-wide knowledge management system to the company's leadership team – start with the new program development VP – with my name next to it*

There was another burst we wanted to add. I've mentioned the fact that we see this future state map as a generic pattern for developing new requirements or new products. Of course, this was the result of the team's increased understanding of the future state map, and we were not sure how the company would react with a proposal of revamping the entire new product development process. So, we considered ourselves like a pilot for the new approach and decided to wait for the results from the implementation to introduce it to the organization.

Detailing the bursts reinforced our belief we have a good grasp on how to fix the current situation and, very importantly, the confirmation that achieving the future state is within our reach, not some mission impossible assignment.

For the summary table for the bursts, please see Appendix F3.

6.5 The Future State Implementation Strategy

Once we understand all the important elements to be implemented and before elaborating the action plan, it's time to look at the implementation strategy – how to proceed with the changes?

In order to help the team settle their ideas, the facilitator might ask questions like the following: what's the best way to introduce this change to the organization? What's the biggest obstacle? What product could benefit from the new approach? Are we going to start implementing all bursts at the same time? What's the time frame we're envisioning? The answers to these questions will shape the implementation approach and then the implementation action plan.

There's no doubt that ensuring full commitment by all the stakeholders before starting the VSM exercise is the preferred way to make sure the action plan will be executed. Remember what Frank had to say on this subject? "There were about seven directors owning different parts of the engineering change process … in the end, they all agreed to invest their people's time not just in participating but in the implementation and sustainment of the improvements too." In case the commitment is not secured up front, the question about obstacles becomes the most important one to answer, because if they are not removed, there's a high risk of not making all the identified changes required to have significant benefits, with a negative impact on the company's business results and on people's engagement in future improvements. It's extremely demotivating for deeply involved participants to see their efforts do not pay off because nothing is implemented.

6.5.1 Time to Practice

Please look at Appendix F3 and Figure 6.5. Both are related to the future state bursts in Ted's story and establish the future state implementation strategy. Then answer the following questions:

- What are the critical elements in the implementation strategy?
- What is the rationale behind your choice?

Let's hear now how Ted and his team went about the future state implementation strategy.

I was really impressed when Frank showed me what was done for the engineering change process, but knowing how things work in our company, I couldn't help asking, "Frank, so all your colleagues are on board with this?" He then gave me more details on the up-front effort he put into getting a commitment from everybody, and this was my starting point for the exercise, so now I was in a good position to start the future state implementation strategy. No major organizational obstacles were expected.

When we asked ourselves the question about what product would benefit from the new approach, we thought of another new product we were developing in parallel, with a new component that required the same type of attention from the safety point of view. Work on the new component hadn't started yet, so this was a good candidate; we just needed to validate with my boss, the new program development VP. We called it PILOT.

Then the facilitator proposed the People – Process – Technology framework to structure our implementation strategy [see Figure 6.6]. What we essentially decided is to group the bursts into the framework categories. This way, bursts A, B, C correspond to people, and we named it "people working together."

Bursts F, G, H correspond to process, and we named it "using the new process." Burst D is complementary to F, G, H, but we wanted to keep it separate although in the same process category. We called it "using the required standards." Burst E corresponds to the technology category, with the name "using the new tool." If we put them side by side and keep the framework order, we have "people working together, using the new process, using the required standards and using the new tool." So, this gave us the implementation order, recognizing we cannot have all of them at the same time. Because there are four elements to be gradually introduced, we ended up with four implementation stages: people working together first stage, using the new process second stage, using the required standards third stage and using the new tool fourth stage. This way, at the end of stage 4, we have all of them up and running. We made a simple table "bursts vs. implementation stage," and we filled it up with the aforementioned elements [black ink, Figure 6.6]. Then we looked at the rows and asked the question: how does this element look at the stages prior to full implementation? Then we wrote the answers in

Future State Bursts	Stage 1	Stage 2	Stage 3	Stage 4
A, B, C	**PEOPLE WORKING TOGETHER**	**PEOPLE WORKING TOGETHER**	**PEOPLE WORKING TOGETHER**	**PEOPLE WORKING TOGETHER**
F, G, H	**IMPLEMENTING THE NEW PROCESS**	**USING THE NEW PROCESS – START**	**USING THE NEW PROCESS**	**USING THE NEW PROCESS**
D	**PRODUCING NEW STANDARDS AS NEEDED**	**PRODUCING NEW STANDARDS AS NEEDED**	**USING THE REQUIRED STANDARDS**	**USING THE REQUIRED STANDARDS**
E	**USING TEMPORARY TOOL, ESTABLISH REQUIREMENTS NEW TOOL**	**USING TEMPORARY TOOL, CHOOSING NEW TOOL**	**USING TEMPORARY TOOL, INSTALLING NEW TOOL**	**USING THE NEW TOOL**

Figure 6.6 Implementation Strategy for the Future State VSM, Critical Component Requirements to Supplier.

gray [gray ink, Figure 6.6]. For instance, F, G, H before "using the new process" requires an intermediary stage of "implementing the new process." Same for D, before "using the required standards," there's a need for "producing new standards, as needed."

Once we completed the table, we had a full picture of the work to be done in each implementation stage. Let's take stage 1, for example: people working together, implementing the new process, producing new standards as needed, using the temporary tool and establishing requirements for the new tool. What this means is we need to have the new team working together ASAP (see the proposal for bursts A, B, C in Appendix F3). In the beginning, they are dedicated to the implementation of the new process (see the proposal for bursts F, G, H in Appendix F3) and the writing of the standards to be used for the PILOT. They are using a temporary tool, and they establish the requirements for the new KM tool. Stage 1 ends when the dedicated multifunction team fully operates in the new way, using the commitment-based scheduling board and when we have the new process defined and ready to be executed. In order to familiarize ourselves with how the board works, we decided to use it for scheduling the execution of stage 1. We knew we couldn't start directly working on the PILOT – that would happen at stage 2, when we execute the new process using the temporary tool and make standards as we need them. Of course, we needed some extra help to succeed, but proceeding this way is a reasonable strategy; we couldn't wait to have all prepared in advance in order to execute. After all, once the elements are in place, all the new programs could potentially benefit because the new approach is already tested.

We gave ourselves a realistic time line of one month for stage 1 and six months overall. Effectively working on PILOT would take five months, which extends our future state time line by half of a month.

6.6 The Value Stream Improvement Action Plan

Defining the future state implementation strategy is greatly helping to define the time line and the order in which the detailed actions need to be executed. The actions are derived from the summary table detailing the bursts. They need to be specific enough to take out all ambiguity related to what needs to be done, to have a clear time frame and a person responsible for the execution.

Let's hear what Ted has to say about the value stream improvement action plan:

At this stage, we went back to the "bursts" summary table [see Appendix F3], derived the concrete actions and started a new table, which includes the description, the responsible person and the time line, arranging them to match the implementation strategy. Then we draw with a red dotted line when we planned to start actual work on PILOT [see Figure 6.7]. This helped us see even better what actions need to be executed prior to the start. As an example, we

	BURST	ACTION DESCRIPTION	RES	TIMELINE [MONTHS]		
				NOW	1	2
D	STANDARDS, KNOWLEDGE STANDARDS	· PERFORM WORKSHOP TO ESTABLISH A LIST OF CRITICAL STANDARDS FOR PILOT	HQ	▉	PILOT START	
		· WRITE CRITICAL STANDARDS NEEDED FOR PILOT	PP	▬▬▬		
		· WRITE STANDARDS AS NEEDED FOR PILOT	PP		▬▬▬▬▬	
F	PROCESS FOR COMPATIBILITY OF MODELS	· PERFORM WORKSHOPS TO SET INSTRUCTIONS ON HOW TO VERIFY IF THE MODELS ARE COMPATIBLE OR NOT, INCLUDING DECISION CRITERIA TO IDENTIFY WHEN AND WHAT CORRECTIONS ARE NECESSARY	DR	▬▬▬		
		· PERFORM TRIALS TO PROVE COMPATIBILITY OF MODELS	ALL	▬▬		
G	THE DOE PROCESS AND DOCUMENT	· WRITE INSTRUCTIONS ON HOW TO SETUP THE DOE AND HOW THE DOE DOCUMENT LOOKS LIKE, INCLUDING INSTRUCTIONS ON HOW TO INTERPRET THE RESULTS AND HOW TO DRAW CONCLUSIONS BASED ON THE RESULTS	HT	▬▬▬		
H	THE CONVERGENCE PROCESS AND DOCUMENT	· WRITE INSTRUCTIONS ON HOW THE CONVERGENCE IS DONE AND HOW THE DOCUMENT LOOKS LIKE, INCLUDING DECISION CRITERIA FOR FINDING THE OPTIMUM ALTERNATIVE	HT	▬▬▬ ?		

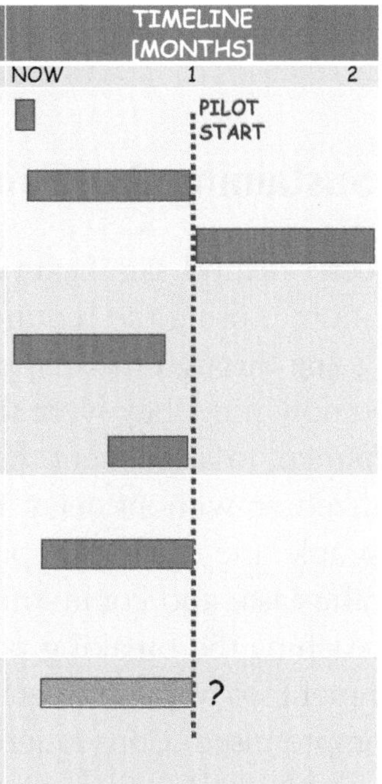

Figure 6.7   Extract from the Implementation Action Plan, Critical Component Requirements to Supplier.

located the convergence process and document at the beginning to be done before starting PILOT, then we realized we're going to need this much later after all the DOE runs are done. However, we left it there because there's a relationship with the DOE process and it is better to work them in parallel. We left the question mark next to it, knowing that our senior INTGR specialist is not part of the multifunction team, so we did not have a full view of her availability, and in case of conflicting priorities, we wanted the DOE process to be done before starting PILOT, with the possibility to do the convergence process at a later date (but not much later than three months after).

As you can see in the table, the team is extremely busy the first month working mainly on the compatibility of models and establishing the critical standards to be used for PILOT. But there's more to be done. We needed others to contribute, so we invited them into the workshop to confirm the actions before putting their names: the senior INTG specialist for the DOE and convergence process, other senior specialists to write the critical standards, HR to formalize the organizational changes and IT to set up the existing business collaboration platform for PILOT use. Not to forget [smiling], this was facilitated by the presence of our new product development VP in the room. Having done the implementation strategy first was a big plus for elaborating the action plan, enabling us to detail tactics while thinking strategically.

For Ted's full value stream implementation action plan, please see Appendix F4. For a complete mapping checklist, please see Appendix A3.

6.7 Sustaining the Gains from the Mapping Exercise

The secret behind significant and sustained improvement is ownership and dedication to bring the required changes to life. By following Ted and the team going through the mapping exercise and looking back at Figure 3.1, we see now how they went through the thought process leading to full commitment to implement the changes. This is something that needs to be capitalized on without delay, right after the exercise. The rule of thumb is very simple: the more time passes by without changing anything, the more the enthusiasm and commitment are fading away (see Figure 6.8). Worse, after reaching the breaking point, people's feelings change to aversion and detachment, so any future attempts to involve them in improvement activities are compromised. Consequently, the best way to capitalize on the dynamic generated in the VSM exercise is to get the team members involved right away in implementing the changes and start living the future state they designed.

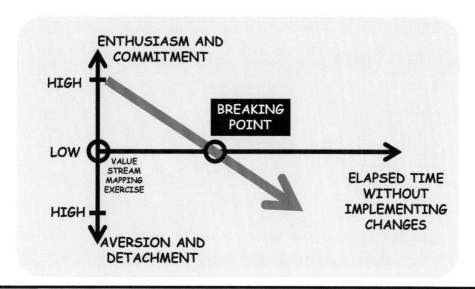

Figure 6.8 Enthusiasm and Commitment vs. Elapsed Time without Implementing Changes.

Conclusion

"The biggest benefit I saw after doing several value stream mapping exercises," says Frank, "is people's engagement. I supported for a long time the thought that people are not coming to work with the goal of doing a bad job; they do their best in an environment setting them up for failure. This leads to disengagement, high people turnover and mediocre business results. Highly engaged teams do wonders. I know this sounds very theoretical but let me give you a real-life example of what engaged people are capable of achieving." Frank continues:

"As I mentioned earlier, I was part of the engineering change process value stream mapping exercise, and I actually led the value stream implementation action plan resulting from it. The problem statement: it takes 173 days for a normal engineering change to be implemented (roughly 6 months). This meant that our new products were delivered with excessive costs, delivered late or with poor quality, and our product upgrades were not keeping pace with the competition. While everybody agreed this is not acceptable, no one was proposing something tangible to get out of the situation. There were at least seven functions involved in the process, each reporting to a different director owning just a chunk and no one owning the whole. It took me several months to convince my peers through targeted one on ones to commit to the change, even though the improvement of the engineering change process was in our yearly business plan."

"Then we had the workshops. What happened during the workshops was extremely rewarding and completely different than the pain we went through the preparation. As we were mapping the current state, you could literally hear pennies dropping as participants started to understand what goes on. The most heard quote was *I can't believe we're doing this to ourselves.* I remember seeing one of the participants taking several pictures from a portion of the map, and when I asked, *So, you're taking souvenirs?* The answer was *not really; I'll use them in my next conversation with my boss; we can't continue this way.* Suddenly it was not just Frank cheerleading for the change but an entire team."

"When we finished mapping the current state and literally run out of wall space, the team decided to use the room as a *shame walk-in*, where leaders and groups of employees were invited to sensitize them to the issue. Team members played the guide role, giving short explanations during the walk while you could see jaws dropping and exclamation signs on invitees' faces. I remember one visiting leader saying *I'm very curious to see what you propose to get us out of this mess*."

"Then it was the first change implementation sprint when we designed and physically put in place the visual management board. Team members were even more into it, as they saw their ideas materialize. While helping cut samples for the cards we were to use, I had a short conversation with a team member that went like this:

"So, Joe, what do you feel about what we're about to do?"

"Frank, to be honest, I thought I have a dull job … crunching numbers day after day, again crunching, then crunching again, I was very seriously considering changing the department when we started all of this … now, I consider I have the best job in the world; I feel my contribution is significant."

"Right after having the visual board on the wall, the team was collocated next to it and started working the new way. Was it perfect? Of course not! Even if the leadership committed up front, there were still some team members who were not entirely dedicated. There was still some running around happening. But we kept at it and finally succeeded in achieving what was thought to be impossible."

"We went from a six-month lead time to a one-month lead time, a reduction of 85%. And it's not just that. A couple of years later, I visited them. They physically changed their location at least three times; their leadership team changed several times, but they maintained the gains. They were proudly showing me the improvements they brought to the board and the ideas they had to improve it further. One friend of mine took me aside and shared with me: *"You know Frank, remember the project manager that used to coordinate the engineering changes before? You know, the one nobody wanted to talk with because of his bitterness and aggressivity … yeah, the one that used to complain all the time in the workshops? Well, just ask around; he's a completely different person now, everybody loves him … he's the one leading the improvements."* Frank concludes:

"What a one-month lead time meant for our business? Roughly half of the cost, on-time new product deliveries and beating the competition for product upgrades. This is what a highly engaged team was capable of achieving by untangling their work."

"Benefits? What benefits do you attach to being able to see?" says Denise. "We couldn't see because of the blinkers we were wearing without even knowing. Blinkers built by our company culture, rewarding individual excellence at the expense of group excellence. Yeah, you could tell this is motherhood and apple pie. The CFO gave us a reality check though: writing off millions of dollars is real, and it hurts. Promoting your function's interest to show how excellent you are, at the expense of genuinely working together, is real and lays the foundation for throwing money out the window. Working with scope changes, and people turnaround is very tedious but add to it working with more than a dozen IT, Engineering and Business functions, like IT Project Office, Data Management, Process & Tools, Design Engineering, working with the Software provider, working with the Solution Architect, all exhibiting their own excellence!"

"The value stream mapping exercise opened our eyes. We could clearly see, just by looking at the current state value stream map how dysfunctional we were. That was the start of our healing. We got control over the process and never run into the same situation as with eHOPE."

"I'm happy to say we got the relationship with our suppliers under control," says Claire, "once we implemented the value stream improvement action plan. It's good when you send the check along with apologies for the unpaid invoice, but it's much better when you pay it when it's due [smiling]. The additional benefit is now we know better how our ERP systems works, how the other function's inputs are impacting the other function's views and data. I personally was not aware of the transactions done by Finance, neither by how the POs I was opening integrate the Finance view. It's much clearer now, and we make much less mistakes."

"I think I've already mentioned some of the benefits," says Ted, "while walking you through how we did it. What I wanted to mention though is, it's hard to put a dollar sign next to people's commitment to making changes, and that's the difficulty when leadership starts asking about ROI. One of our leaders asked, '*So, what's the value add of doing the value stream mapping exercise? What am I getting for freeing up my people for this? How much money are we going to save?*' Good questions but totally missing the point and, frankly, disrespectful. We were losing money as we were speaking because of a broken process. It was not about what do I get in return but about what do I have to do to correct this. They just show lack of trust from the leader. People's commitment to making changes led us to completely redesign the way we were establishing requirements and possibly rethinking our entire new program development process for the better. How do you attach money to that?" Ted continues:

"The PILOT was a success. We delivered the requirements on time and without rework. Was it easy? Nope. We stumbled right at the beginning when we tried to reconcile our models. Technical complications due to the various software packages in use made it such that a lot of workarounds needed to be implemented and that slowed us down. We knew we can't just dictate one software for all, so it was people's commitment to making changes that allowed us to advance despite the difficulties. The other one slowing us down was putting together the required knowledge standards because the data we needed was all over the place, so it was hard to gather it. Working on these issues took more time than we thought it's going to take, but we've caught up in the latter part, where the convergence took less time."

"I'll always be thankful to Frank for convincing me to try this approach to value stream mapping; we've accomplished much more than we thought is possible."

Appendix A: VSM Checklists

Appendix A1 The Value Stream Walk Checklist

Appendix A1.1 VS Walk Preparation

Objective: Establish the trajectory and the approximate duration for the VS walk, secure people's availability to answer questions

Preparation questions	Notes
What real-life product we became? (real example)	
What are the product's transformation stages?	
What are the starting and ending points for the product transformation process?	
Who are the stakeholders in this process (functions, departments)?	
Who are the persons to contact, and where are they located?	
How much time can these people dedicate to our inquiries?	

Appendix A1.2 VS Walk Execution

Objective: Get facts and data about the process, observe first-hand how work is performed – no judgment calls, no solutions

Generic Questions for Each Stakeholder	Notes
What's your function?	
What role do you play?	
What product do you touch?	
What tools and databases do you use to transform the product?	
What instructions do you use to transform the product?	
What information do you need to transform the product?	
Who provides the information to you?	
What's your trigger to transform the product?	
What do you deliver?	

Generic Questions for Each Stakeholder	*Notes*
Who needs what you deliver?	
What are the main activities you perform?	
Are there any other persons performing the same activities?	
How long does it typically take from receiving the information to delivering it?	
Is historical data concerning the times available?	
What are the main issues you're facing?	
Is historical data concerning the issues available?	
What constraints are you dealing with?	

Appendix A2 The VSM Preparation Checklist

Questions for Preparation	*Notes*
What's the business pain?	
Who's the owner?	
Who's the champion?	
Who are the small team members (names and functions)?	
What's today's business context around the business pain?	
What are the past attempts to fix the business pain?	
What are the current initiatives to deal with the business pain?	
Who needs to be engaged?	
How are we going to engage them?	
What's the problem statement?	
What's the objective?	
What's the measure?	
What's the product?	
What are the main transformation stages for the product?	
What's the link with the final product?	
What's the impact on the paying customer?	
What's the real-life example?	
What's the trajectory for the VS walk?	
Who to visit during the VS walk?	
How much time for the VS walk?	
Did the required people confirm we can see them during the VS walk?	
What are the observations made during the VS walk?	
What are the collected artifacts during the VS walk?	
What does the VS walk report out look like?	
Who are the large team members (names and functions)?	
Did all the required stakeholders commit?	
Were all required stakeholders invited to the workshop?	

Appendix A3 The Current and Future VSM Checklist

Mapping Questions	Notes
CURRENT STATE	
Mapping conventions and icons explained?	
A-B-C demonstration with a simple example made?	
Does the high-level current state map have all the required A-B-C elements?	
Were the conventions respected for the high-level current state map?	
Does the detailed-level current state map have all the required A-B-C elements?	
Were the conventions respected for the detailed-level current state map?	
Was the count of icons for the detailed level current state map done?	
Was the summary table cause and adverse effect done?	
Is the rework detail table done?	
Were the information flow patterns in the detailed-level current state map identified?	
Is a 5 Whys root cause analysis necessary? If yes – was it performed?	
Are the current state map conclusions summarized?	
FUTURE STATE	
Is the future state criteria done?	
Is the technical backbone done?	
Do all understand how the Waste Machine works?	
Do all understand how to deal with the Waste Machine?	
Were the new icons explained?	
Is the future state strategy done?	
Does the high-level future state map have all the required A-B-C elements?	
Does the detailed-level future state map have all the required A-B-C elements?	
VERIFICATION AND IMPROVEMENT ACTION PLAN	
Did we run a simulation through the future state map?	
Did we quantify the before and after?	
Did we check the future state map against the future state criteria?	
Are adjustments to the future state map necessary?	
Were the future state map bursts identified?	
Is the future state implementation strategy done?	
Is the value stream improvement action plan done?	
Is ownership established and embraced?	

Appendix B: Icons Used for VSM

Appendix B1 Current and Future State VSM Icons, Activities Flow

Icon	Description	Use
ACTIVITY SHORT DESCRIPTION ACTIVITY	The activity box icon. Contains a brief description of the activity performed, two to five words max. It includes at the minimum a verb and a noun. Examples: *Create PO, Modify Drawing, Write Code, Perform XYZ Analysis*. Activity boxes can be placed in series, in parallel, using bifurcations or collectors, according to how the process is executed.	Activity flow, black ink
PEOPLE FUNCTION NUMBER	People performing the activity icon. Contains the name of the function performing the respective activity, along with a distinctive number. This distinctive number reflects the number of different persons from the same function that are executing activities. For instance, if there are two people from purchasing who perform the same activity, there should be two icons, one with Purchasing 1 and the other with Purchasing 2 at the bottom. The icon should be used each time a new function intervenes or when a previously captured function intervenes again after another function.	Activity flow, black ink
OTHERS	Others icon. Represents other people touching the product but not transforming it. For example, status meetings where the product is touched with regards to the transformation stage, but there's no activity to transform the product.	Activity flow, black ink

Icon	Description	Use
6 NUMBER OF DISTINCTIVE PEOPLE	Number of people icon. Distinctive number of people touching the product from the beginning to the end. It reflects each new person touching the product and is positioned against each people performing the activities icon. Caution: persons touching the product could be a much bigger number than persons actually transforming the product. For instance, someone transporting the product or receiving status about the product count as touching the product, but not transforming it. Example: if there is a total of ten activities performed by three functions, each function using two people, the distinctive number of people touching the product is six. So, for this example, there's going to be blue numbers from one to six against each distinctive people.	Activity flow, highlight, blue ink
TURNING POINT	Turning point icon. A turning point is the activity that made a difference in executing the captured process in a positive way. As the mapping exercise unfolds, the turning points need to be captured next to the corresponding activities. Used for capturing the current state, it is an element to be considered when designing the future state.	Activity flow, highlight, blue ink
ITERATIONS	Iterations icon. Highlights activities that are part of iterations to differentiate them from rework. Mainly used in design processes. Associated with the circle icon.	Activity flow, highlight, blue ink
CIRCLE	Circle icon. Used to circle activities or group of activities in order to highlight a certain condition. For example, we can circle a portion of a high level VSM in order to indicate that we are zooming in that area with a detailed VSM. In this case, we indicate with blue ink next to the circle the title of the detailed VSM.	Activity flow, highlight, blue ink
PUSH	Push arrow icon. Links the activities and denotes a push way of working when the previous activity releases work without considering the subsequent activity's capability of absorbing it. One can use the bidirectional arrow for pushing back and forth between functions. Sometimes called "throw over the fence," this is characteristic of a batch and queue operation. In a batch and queue operation, there's an accumulation of work between functions, creating inventory, wait times that contribute to overall long lead times, to quality issues and to higher costs. It helps identify indirectly the waste of waiting and inventory.	Activity flow, black ink

Icon	Description	Use
ENTITY	Entity icon. Delimits the physical entities contributing to the process. Could be supplier or customer, could be different locations like *San Diego facility, Tokyo office, Berlin warehouse*. The same icon can be used for delimiting the activities taking place within a function. These entities can capture their internal activities, or they can be just linked by the information flow.	Activity flow, black ink
FRUSTRATION	Frustration icon. Represented as a dark cloud, it is associated with people's frustration in different situations. It is mainly associated with the information flow being generated in meetings, discussions, chases. It is located above the people, discussion or meetings icons.	No particular flow, black ink
	Box, black dotted line icon. Circles several activities with the meaning that only one activity from all the circled ones could happen at a time. It helps saving space when mapping and is associated with the activity icon.	Activities flow, black ink
	Box, blue dotted line icon. Circles the sequence of activities managed by visual management. It is associated with the visual board icon and with the activity icon.	Activities flow, blue ink
VISUAL BOARD	Visual board icon. Represents the place where we can see the advancement of the product's transformation or the advancement of tasks in real time. Used for planning and for highlighting abnormalities needing resolution. Usually used by a multifunction team. Associated with the box, blue dotted line icon, it is placed above the activities managed by it.	Information flow, black ink, trigger *(exception to the color rule – black ink used to show a physical place)*
FLOW REGULATOR	The flow regulator icon. Controlled point that dictates the flow rate to the rest of the process; it could be one (recommended) or several in the case when full continuity cannot be achieved. It is placed next to the activity icon representing the control point. Associated with the FIFO (the entry activity for FIFO) and information supermarket icons (the activity that consumes from the supermarket).	Activity flow, highlight, blue ink

Icon	Description	Use
BURST	Burst icon. Used to highlight the future state elements that need to be implemented for the future state to work. It's the basis for the future state action plan. A letter is used to make the connection with the item in the action plan. Placed next to the future state element, which can be in the information or in the activity flow.	No particular flow, green

Appendix B2 Current and Future State VSM Icons, Information Flow

Icon	Description	Use
INBOX	The inbox icon. Virtual communication environment, which needs checking and manipulation in order to see and act upon the content. The inbox is the component of the information flow where both information and triggers accumulate. It helps with capturing waste of inventory.	Information flow, red ink
EMAIL / EMAIL WITH ATTACHMENT	The email icon. Virtual communication vehicle, which needs checking and manipulation in order to see and act upon the content. Could be simple or with attachments. The email is the component of the information flow where information resides and could become a trigger to perform work. Example: *I start working on something when I receive the email asking me to do so; I start working when I receive your file (email attachment).* It helps with capturing waste of transportation.	Information flow, red ink, trigger
DATABASE NAME	Database icon. Virtual information and data storage environment, which needs checking and manipulation in order to store, to modify or to retrieve content. The database icon can be used to represent automated workflow systems. Examples: ERP (SAP, QAD, etc.), ACCESS, C: drive, eROOM, ENOVIA, Outlook. It helps with capturing waste of inventory.	Information flow, red ink

Icon	Description	Use
DOCUMENT NAME .extension	Document icon. Virtual place where data and information reside, which needs checking and manipulation in order to see and act upon the content. Documents could be drawings, reports, memos, presentations, etc., and can be associated with emails as attachments, databases as where they are stored, checks, information and data manipulation icons. Examples extensions: *.doc, .xls, .pdf, .catproduct, .catpart, .ppt.* It helps with capturing waste of overprocessing or inventory.	Information flow, red ink
CHECK	Check icon. The check icon is used whenever the information is looked for, assessed, validated, analyzed, evaluated, verified, etc., and is part of the information flow. It involves reliance on the individual's judgment to process the information. Could be placed next to activity boxes, inboxes, emails, documents, databases. It helps with capturing waste of overprocessing.	Information flow, red ink
INFO, DATA MANIPU LATION	Information or data manipulation icon. It reflects manual processing of information or data, heavily reliant on people's attention or skills. Could be manual entries in information systems, writing emails, attaching files to emails, making drawings, altering models, checking boxes in workflows or selecting items from drop-down menus. Could be placed next to activity boxes, inboxes, emails, documents, etc. and helps with capturing waste of overprocessing.	Information flow, red ink
WAITING	Waiting icon. Shows the places where there's a pause in a product's transformation, for various reasons. Could be placed next to inboxes, if the email is not read for a significant period of time, between activities if there's a significant lapse of time between their execution. Other examples: waiting for a response, waiting for approval. The waiting reason is typically captured in a red cloud next to the icon. It helps with capturing waste of waiting.	Information flow, red ink

Icon	Description	Use
ISSUE (cloud icon) ISSUE (cloud icon)	Issue icon. Captures the issues encountered while executing the process. A short description of the issue is written in the cloud, which is placed next to where it occurred. The captured issues need to be factually based. Issues could be activity related (black ink) or information flow related (red ink). Some examples: "busy schedules" cloud next to the waiting icon, "no follow-up" cloud next to the phone call icon, "short of licenses" cloud next to the software icon, "wrong meshing" next to the activity icon. For big issues, the cloud can be accentuated to stand out. It helps with capturing failure modes and waste of defects.	Information flow, red ink, Activity, black ink
TIME BOMB (bomb icon) BOOM 6 (explosion icon)	Time bomb and boom icons. They help with capturing failure mechanisms. Capture the relationship between a cause and its adverse effect, usually separated by a long period of time. The time bomb is placed next to the activity where the spark originates and the boom icon next to the activity where the adverse effect became obvious. Numbers can be used to differentiate between several cause and adverse effect situations and a three-column summary table can be used on a separate sheet to compile them (description, what was the cause – time bomb, what was the adverse effect – boom). Can be associated with issue or rework icons. Example: using the wrong data for performing a particular analysis (time bomb) resulted in redoing the analysis when we later verified the data source and realized it was not good (boom). It helps with capturing failure modes and waste of defects.	Information flow, red ink

Icon	Description	Use
REWORK (icon with number 6)	Rework icon. Shows the place where a return in the process was triggered. Numbers can be used to differentiate between several rework loops and a three-column summary table can be used on a separate sheet to compile them (description, details). A cloud next to it specifying "back to … " can indicate the return activity in the process. Can be associated with the boom icon. It helps with capturing waste of defects.	Information flow, red ink, yellow background
SCHEDULE (calendar icon)	Schedule icon. Virtual place, usually a Microsoft Project file where activities and the respective due dates reside. Schedules are usually presented and tracked in governance reviews by project people and can become triggers to perform work. They are part of the information flow and are frequently associated with the check, issue and chaser icons.	Information flow, red ink, trigger
SOFTWARE NAME (monitor icon)	Software icon. Shows what specialized software is used to perform activities. Part of the information flow, it gives an indication on the required knowledge to perform them. It is placed next to the activity icon. Examples: *Matlab, CATIA, NASTRAN.*	Information flow, red ink
WORKFLOW (filmstrip icon)	Workflow icon. Information system that manages work task by task by sending signals to users asking for intervention in the system. When receiving the signal, the user is supposed to enter the system and perform a certain task, which becomes then the signal to perform a task for another user in the predetermined sequence. Associated with the database icon and with the information path icon.	Information flow, red ink, trigger
PRINTER (printer icon)	Printer icon. Physical place where the information or data is made available in physical form. It can be placed next to the activity icon and can become a trigger to perform work.	Information flow, red ink, trigger

Icon	Description	Use
INFORMATION PATH	Information path icon. Links map components to show how they connect with each other. The arrow points into the direction of the recipient. Example: an arrow linking a document with a database pointing toward the database means the document is stored in the database; pointing to the document means the document is retrieved from the database.	Information flow, red ink
PEOPLE INFO	People information icon. It's a person becoming part of the information flow. When a person has information that is not available to others, it becomes the only means by which the respective information can be shared. It depends on the willingness and interests of that person if the information is shared or not, if it is distorted or not, with consequences on the process execution. Example: if a person verbally distributing jobs to others is sick, the jobs are not performed. Helps recording organizational politics, decision-making. It can be associated with frustration, callout, activity, time bomb icons and can become a trigger to perform work. It helps with identifying failure modes and behavioral patterns.	Information flow, red ink, trigger
TEXT HERE CALLOUT TEXT HERE CALLOUT	Callout icon. Captures the essential message made by a person in the information flow, be it individually, be it part of a discussion or part of a meeting. Helps completing a situation by giving details, personalizing it. The red callout icon can be used for very important messages. It can be associated with people info, discussion, meeting, chaser icons.	Information flow, red ink

Icon	Description	Use
DISCUSSION VERBAL TEXT PHONE CALL VIDEO CALL IM-INSTANT MESSAGING	Discussion icon. Verbal or electronic exchange or generation of information in an informal way (corridor discussions, text messages, phone calls) involving two or more people. Usually there's no artifact of the exchanged information, which remains with the participants in the discussion. It depends on the people's willingness and interests if the respective information is shared or not if it's kept the same or distorted and how it is shared. The outcome of the discussion is open to interpretation and dependent on participants' perceptions, biases and emotions. As part of the information flow, it helps record conflicting situations, clarifications, updates on different topics, organizational politics, decision-making and can become a trigger to perform work. It can be associated with the frustration, cloud, activity, time bomb and callout icons. It helps with identifying failure modes and behavioral patterns.	Information flow, red ink, trigger
MEETING CONF ROOM CONF CALL VIDEO CONF VIDEO CALL	Meeting icon. Formal way of exchanging or generating information between two or more participants, via different means: in a conference room, over the phone, over a video system, over video chat applications. They can be on a recurring (daily/weekly/monthly) or not recurring, as-needed basis. Holding a meeting involves coordination work by an organizer and is highly dependent on the number of invitees, their availability and their group's priorities. More people required, more difficult to find common free time slots, so several back-and-forth rounds are usually required to accommodate everybody. Preparation is usually required; the organizer needs to prepare an agenda and to make sure the ones required to present will have their material available in advance. Despite the preparation work, low attendance is possible because priorities change rapidly or emergencies pop up without warning, hurting the exchange of information and the outcome of the	Information flow, red ink, trigger

Icon	Description	Use
	meeting. Meeting facilitation is very important for sharing the information the right way and is dependent on how the organizer handles the crowd. The usual outcomes of the meeting are the minutes of the meeting and the action plan, all recorded and shared afterward by the organizer. They are highly dependent on the organizer's skills, participant's preparation and involvement. Part of the information flow, it helps record conflicting situations, clarifications, updates on different topics, decision-making, organizational politics and can become a trigger to perform work. It can be associated with activity, inbox, email, document, callout, frustration, cloud, time bomb icons. It helps with identifying failure modes, waste of overprocessing and behavioral patterns.	
NAME HANDING PAPER DOCUMENT	Handing paper icon. Exchange of information through the means of a paper document between two or more people, which needs checking and manipulation in order to hand/receive, to see and act upon the content. The exchange is highly dependent on the one printing and handing the document, also on the recipient's handling or storage of the document. Part of the information flow, it can be associated with activity, checking, callout, frustration, cloud, time bomb, chaser icons. It can become a trigger to perform work, and it helps recording failure modes and waste of overprocessing.	Information flow, red ink, trigger
CHASER	Chaser icon. It's a person looking for information or pushing other people to generate information (documents, drawings, etc.). The chaser is part of the information flow and links the source with the consumer and implies the link between them does not exist or is extremely difficult to establish. Typically, the chaser is part of a project team but can be a part of any other group or a part of management too. It can be associated with activity, checking, callout, frustration, cloud, time bomb icons. Usually, it's a trigger to perform work, and it helps recording failure modes, waste of overprocessing and behavioral patterns.	Information flow, red ink, trigger

Icon	Description	Use
F I F O	First-in-First-Out (FIFO) icon regulates the consumer – supplying activities with the goal of processing information one at a time, in the arrival order and with a finite backlog in the pipeline; this ensures seamless processing, with a controlled inventory of information in between. It is placed above the activities flow, starting from the supplying activity and ending with the consuming activity.	
INFORMATION SUPERMARKET	The information supermarket icon. Regulates the consumer – supplying activities and works on the principle "take one, put one back" – processing information one at a time, so as we consume one piece of information, the one supplying needs to make available other information; this ensures seamless processing and making sure the information is not generated too early, with the risk of becoming out-of-date. It is placed between the supplying and consuming activities.	Information flow, red ink, trigger

Appendix C: Detailed Current State VSM for *Wrong Requirements for Critical Component Sent to Supplier, New Product Development* (Ted's Story)

Appendix C1 Sheet 1

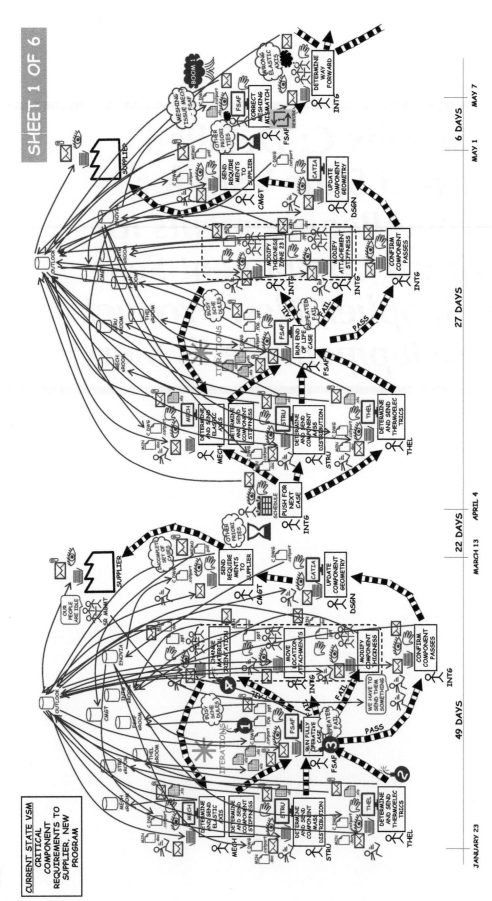

Appendix C2 Sheet 2

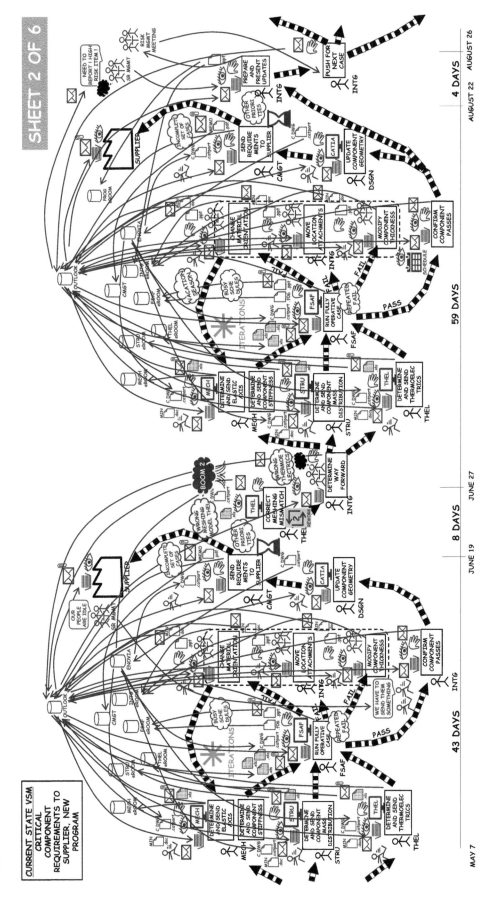

Appendix C3 Sheet 3

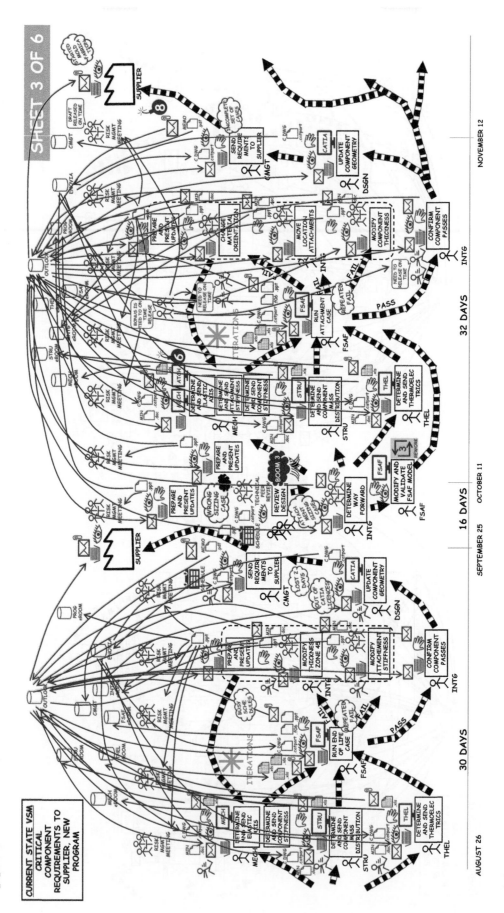

Appendix C4 Sheet 4

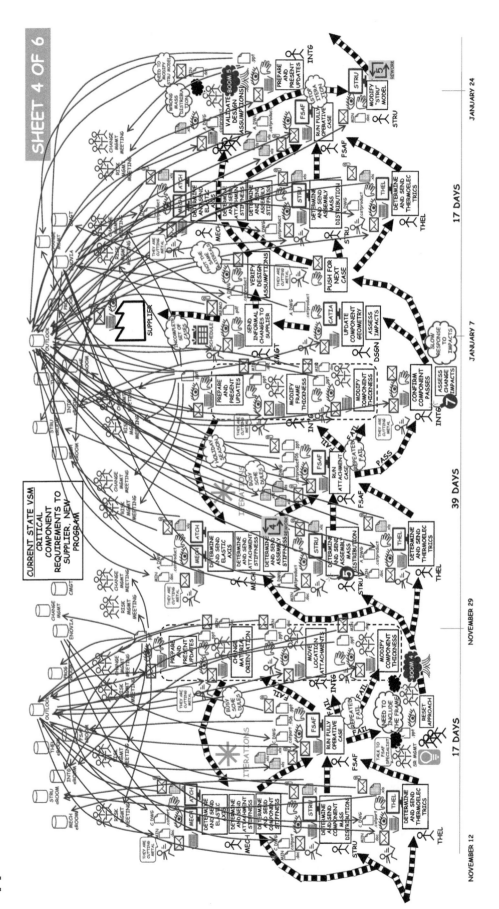

Appendix C5 Sheet 5

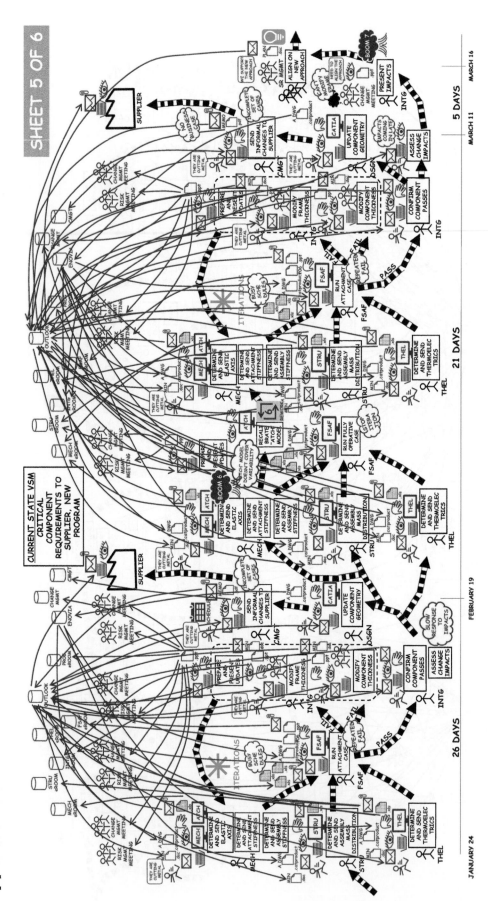

Appendix C6 Sheet 6

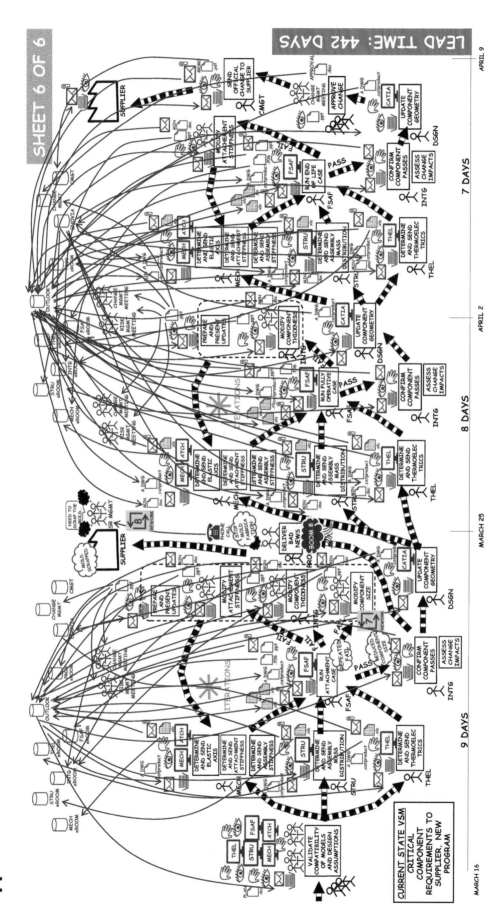

Appendix D: Conclusions Current State VSM for *Wrong Requirements for Critical Component Sent to Supplier, New Product Development* (Ted's Story)

Appendix D1 Summary Icons

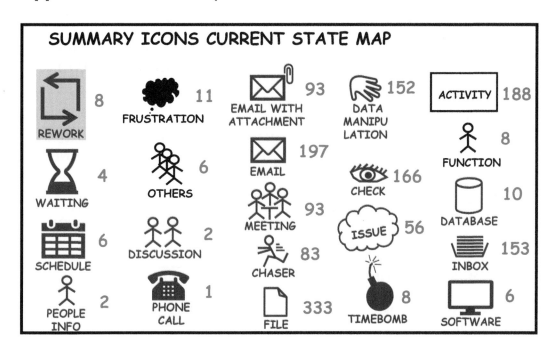

Appendix D2 Cause & Adverse Effect Summary Table

	VISIBLE CAUSE	ADVERSE EFFECT	IMPACTS
1	USE OF THE FSAF MODEL WITHOUT BEING RECONCILED WITH THE MECH MODEL. MESHING MISMATCH.	REALIZATION THAT UNTIL THEN WE WORKED WITH THE WRONG ELASTIC AXIS.	ALL ANALYSIS DONE SO FAR NOT GOOD, NEED TO RESTART THE ANALYSIS CYCLE FROM THE BEGINNING. DELAYS AND REWORK.
2	MESHING ERROR IN THE THEL MODEL. WRONG REPRESENTATION IN THE FSAF MODEL.	REALIZATION THAT UNTIL THEN WE WERE WORKING WITH THE WRONG THERMOELECTRIC DISTRIBUTION.	ALL ANALYSIS DONE SO FAR NOT GOOD, NEED TO RESTART THE ANALYSIS CYCLE FROM THE BEGINNING. DELAYS AND REWORK.
3	SIZING CASE NOT WELL IDENTIFIED AT THE BEGINNING.	REALIZATION THAT UNTIL THEN WE WERE USING THE WRONG SIZING CASE.	ALL ANALYSIS DONE SO FAR NOT GOOD, NEED TO RESTART THE ANALYSIS CYCLE FROM THE BEGINNING. DELAYS AND REWORK.
4	LEVERS NOT WELL IDENTIFIED AT THE BEGINNING. SEE ASSEMBLY VS COMPONENT CONSIDERATIONS.	REALIZATION THAT UNTIL THEN WE WERE USING THE WRONG LEVERS TO SECURE A SAFE COMPONENT DESIGN.	SAFE COMPONENT DESIGN NOT ACHIEVED. DELAYS AND REWORK.
5	MASS DISTRIBUTION FOR THE FRAME CALCULATED WITH THE WRONG TYPE OF MATERIAL.	REALIZATION THAT SINCE THE NEW APPROACH STARTED, WE WERE WORKING WITH THE WRONG DESIGN ASSUMPTION INVOLVING THE FRAME MATERIAL.	ALL ANALYSIS DONE SO FAR NOT GOOD, NEED TO RESTART THE ANALYSIS CYCLE FROM THE BEGINNING. DELAYS AND REWORK.
6	USE OF THE ATCH MODEL WITHOUT MAKING SURE IT COVERS THE VARIABILITY.	REALIZATION THAT SINCE THE NEW APPROACH STARTED, WE WERE WORKING WITH A WRONGLY CALIBRATED ATCH MODEL.	WRONG DATA GENERATED. DELAYS AND REWORK.
7	CONTINUE TO MODIFY THE FRAME WITH INCOMPLETE CHANGE IMPACT ASSESSMENT.	LATE REALIZATION THAT IT IS TOO COSTLY TO MODIFY THE FRAME.	RESTART THE ANALYSIS CYCLE BY MODIFYING THE COMPONENT. DELAYS AND REWORK.

	VISIBLE CAUSE	ADVERSE EFFECT	IMPACTS
8	THE REQUIREMENTS THAT WERE USED TO START THE MOLD FABRICATION WERE SENT WITHOUT "PASS" FROM ALL THE REQUIRED CASES BEFORE THE APPROACH WAS RESET TO COVER WORKING WITH THE ASSEMBLY.	REALIZATION THAT THE CORRESPONDING DIMENSIONS OF A SAFE COMPONENT DESIGN REQUIRE SCRAPPING THE CURRENT, VERY EXPENSIVE MOLD THE SUPPLIER WAS MACHINING.	SCRAPPED MOLD. REWORK, DELAYS AND DIRECT COST OVERRUNS.

Appendix D3 Rework Table

	REWORK DETAILS
REWORK	
1	CORRECTING THE MESHING MISMATCH BETWEEN THE MECH MODEL AND THE FSAF MODEL BY MODIFYING THE FSAF MODEL.
2	CORRECTING THE MESHING MISMATCH BETWEEN THE THEL MODEL AND THE FSAF MODEL BY MODIFYING THE THEL MODEL.
3	MODIFYING THE FSAF MODEL TO INCLUDE INPUTS FROM THE ATCH MODEL, REQUIRED TO RUN THE TRUE SIZING CASE.
4	HAVING TO RECONSIDER THE APPROACH: WORKING WITH THE ASSEMBLY INSTEAD OF WORKING WITH JUST THE COMPONENT.
5	MODIFYING THE STRU MODEL TO INCLUDE THE TRUE TYPE OF THE FRAME MATERIAL.
6	RECALIBRATING THE ATCH MODEL TO COVER THE VARIABILITY CALLED BY THE TRUE SIZING CASE.
7	HAVING TO RECONSIDER THE APPROACH: MODIFYING THE COMPONENT INSTEAD OF MODIFYING THE FRAME.
8	HAVING TO RESTART FABRICATION OF A NEW MOLD.

Appendix D4 Conclusion Statements

CONCLUSIONS CURRENT STATE VSM CRITICAL COMPONENT REQUIREMENTS TO SUPPLIER
- IT TOOK 442 DAYS TO RELEASE MATURE COMPONENT REQUIREMENTS
- WE WORK IN AN INBOX TO INBOX AND MEETING-TO-MEETING ENVIRONMENT
- MINIMUM 290 EMAILS FOR 188 ACTIVITIES – EXCESSIVE RELIANCE ON EMAILS

- MINIMUM 93 MEETINGS FOR 188 ACTIVITIES – EXCESSIVE GOVERNANCE, DECISION BY COMMITTEE
- WE WORK IN SILOS
- DIFFERENT FUNCTIONS HAVE DIFFERENT PRIORITIES – 13 RECORDED ISSUES FOR 188 ACTIVITIES RELATED TO PRIORITIES
- CHASING IS THE MAIN MEAN TO ADVANCE WORK – MINIMUM 83 CHASING SITUATIONS FOR 188 ACTIVITIES
- PEOPLE DRIVEN PROCESS, PRONE TO ERRORS
- MINIMUM 152 DATA MANIPULATION INSTANCES AND 166 CHECKING INSTANCES FOR 188 ACTIVITIES
- 8 MAJOR REWORK RECORDED DUE TO TECHNICAL AND MODELING ERRORS
- HEAVY RELIANCE ON EXPERTS FOR TECHNICAL JUDGMENT – SEE THE WRONG SIZING CASE, THE ASSEMBLY VS COMPONENT APPROACH
- NO VISIBILITY ON THE OVERALL ADVANCEMENT – THE ONLY VISIBILITY IS ON WHAT ITERATION WE'RE IN NOW – WE LIVE FROM ONE ITERATION TO ANOTHER
- IT ALL STARTED ON THE WRONG FOOT – FOUR OUT OF EIGHT TIME BOMBS ARE LOCATED AT THE BEGINNING
- WE'RE IN A FULL PUSH SYSTEM WITH ACCUMULATIONS AND RETURNS, THERE'S NO FLOW – SEE PUSH ARROWS
- PREVALENT TYPES OF WASTE GENERATED BY THE WAY WE WORK ARE: WAITING, DEFECTS AND OVERPROCESSING
- MISALIGNED LEADERSHIP TEAM – THINGS IMPROVED ONCE THE LEADERSHIP ALIGNMENT FOR THE NEW APPROACH WAS MADE
- MOVING ON WITH OPEN KNOWLEDGE GAPS – SEE THE WRONG SIZING CASE, THE ASSEMBLY VS COMPONENT APPROACH, INCOMPLETE IMPACTS ANALYSIS REGARDING THE FRAME, THE USE OF THE ATCH MODEL

Appendix E: Preparation Future State VSM for *Wrong Requirements for Critical Component Sent to Supplier, New Product Development* (Ted's Story)

Appendix E1 Criteria Future State

CRITERIA FUTURE STATE VSM CRITICAL COMPONENT REQUIREMENTS TO SUPPLIER

- [ ] LESS THAN 221 DAYS TO RELEASE MATURE COMPONENT REQUIREMENTS
- [ ] LESS RELIANCE ON EMAILS, MEETINGS AND CHASING TO ADVANCE WORK
- [ ] ALL STAKEHOLDERS HAVE ALIGNED PRIORITIES
- [ ] ERROR PROOF PROCESS, LESS ERRORS
- [ ] REAL TIME VISIBILITY ON THE OVERALL ADVANCEMENT
- [ ] PROACTIVE START OF THE PROCESS
- [ ] ACHIEVE FLOW
- [ ] LEADERSHIP TEAM ALIGNMENT AND RIGHT LEVEL DECISION MAKING

CONCLUSIONS CURRENT STATE VSM	CRITERIA FUTURE STATE VSM	
IT TOOK 442 DAYS TO RELEASE MATURE COMPONENT REQUIREMENTS	LESS THAN 221 DAYS TO RELEASE MATURE COMPONENT REQUIREMENTS	1
WE WORK IN AN INBOX-TO-INBOX AND MEETING-TO-MEETING ENVIRONMENT	LESS RELIANCE ON EMAILS, MEETINGS AND CHASING TO ADVANCE WORK	2
MINIMUM 290 EMAILS FOR 188 ACTIVITIES - EXCESSIVE RELIANCE ON EMAILS	LESS EMAILS	2
MINIMUM 93 MEETINGS FOR 188 ACTIVITIES - EXCESSIVE GOVERNANCE. DECISION BY COMMITTEE	RIGHT LEVEL FOR DECISION MAKING	9
WE WORK IN SILOES	NO MORE WORKING IN SILOES	3
DIFFERENT FUNCTIONS HAVE DIFFERENT PRIORITIES - 13 RECORDED ISSUES FOR 188 ACTIVITIES RELATED TO PRIORITIES	ALL STAKEHOLDERS HAVE ALIGNED PRIORITIES	2
CHASING IS THE MAIN MEAN TO ADVANCE WORK - MINIMUM 83 CHASING SITUATIONS FOR 188 ACTIVITIES	NO MORE CHASING	4
PEOPLE DRIVEN PROCESS, PRONE TO ERRORS	ERROR PROOF PROCESS, LESS ERRORS	4
MINIMUM 152 DATA MANIPULATION INSTANCES AND 166 CHECKING INSTANCES FOR 188 ACTIVITIES	LESS DATA MANIPULATION AND LESS CHECKING	4
EIGHT MAJOR REWORK RECORDED DUE TO TECHNICAL AND MODELING ERRORS	NO MORE MAJOR REWORK DUE TO TECHNICAL AND MODELING ERRORS	4
HEAVY RELIANCE ON EXPERTS FOR TECHNICAL JUDGEMENT - SEE THE WRONG SIZING CASE, THE ASSEMBLY VS COMPONENT APPROACH	LESS RELIANCE ON EXPERTS FOR TECHNICAL JUDGEMENT	5
NO VISIBILITY ON THE OVERALL ADVANCEMENT - THE ONLY VISIBILITY IS ON WHAT ITERATION WE'RE IN NOW - WE LIVE FROM ONE ITERATION TO ANOTHER	REAL TIME VISIBILITY ON THE OVERALL ADVANCEMENT	6
IT ALL STARTED ON THE WRONG FOOT - FOUR OUT OF EIGHT TIMEBOMBS ARE LOCATED AT THE BEGINNING	PROACTIVE START OF THE PROCESS	7
WE'RE IN A FULL PUSH SYSTEM WITH ACCUMULATIONS AND RETURNS. THERE'S NO FLOW - SEE PUSH ARROWS	ACHIEVE FLOW	7
PREVALENT TYPES OF WASTE GENERATED BY THE WAY WE WORK ARE: WAITING, DEFECTS AND OVERPROCESSING	LESS WAITING, DEFECTS AND OVERPROCESSING	8
MISALIGNED LEADERSHIP TEAM - THINGS IMPROVED ONCE THE LEADERSHIP ALIGNMENT FOR THE NEW APPROACH WAS MADE	LEADERSHIP TEAM ALIGNMENT AND RIGHT LEVEL DECISION MAKING	7
MOVING ON WITH OPEN KNOWLEDGE GAPS - SEE THE WRONG SIZING CASE, THE ASSEMBLY VS COMPONENT APPROACH. INCOMPLETE IMPACTS ANALYSIS REGARDING THE FRAME, THE USE OF THE ATCH MODEL	TIMELY CLOSURE OF KNOWLEDGE GAPS	7

Appendix E2 Technical Backbone

TECHNICAL BACKBONE – BEFORE (1) AND AFTER (2), CRITICAL COMPONENT REQUIREMENTS TO SUPPLIER

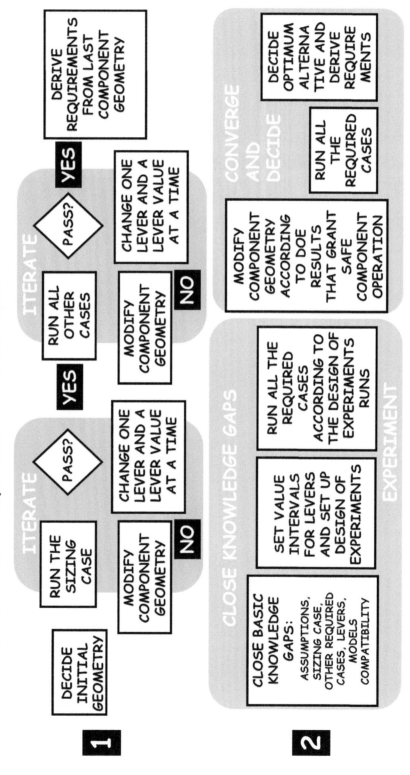

Appendix F: Verification and Implementation Action Plan Future State VSM for *Wrong Requirements for Critical Component Sent to Supplier, New Product Development* (Ted's Story)

Appendix F1 Future State Elements That Address Causes (Amended Cause & Adverse Effect Summary Table)

	VISIBLE CAUSE	ADVERSE EFFECT	ADDRESSED BY THE FUTURE STATE
1	USE OF THE FSAF MODEL WITHOUT BEING RECONCILED WITH THE MECH MODEL. MESHING MISMATCH.	REALIZATION THAT UNTIL THEN WE WORKED WITH THE WRONG ELASTIC AXIS.	YES – SEE THE ACTIVITY VERIFY AND VALIDATE COMPATIBILITY OF MODELS, DONE UP FRONT Figure 5.13.
2	MESHING ERROR IN THE THEL MODEL. WRONG REPRESENTATION IN THE FSAF MODEL.	REALIZATION THAT UNTIL THEN WE WERE WORKING WITH THE WRONG THERMOELECTRIC DISTRIBUTION.	YES – SEE THE ACTIVITY VERIFY AND VALIDATE COMPATBILITY OF MODELS, DONE UP FRONT Figure 5.13.

	VISIBLE CAUSE	ADVERSE EFFECT	ADDRESSED BY THE FUTURE STATE
3	SIZING CASE NOT WELL IDENTIFIED AT THE BEGINNING.	REALIZATION THAT UNTIL THEN WE WERE USING THE WRONG SIZING CASE.	YES – SEE THE ACTIVITY DECIDE SIZING CASE AND OTHER CASES, DONE UP FRONT AND USING LIMIT CURVES AND STANDARDS Figure 5.13.
4	LEVERS NOT WELL IDENTIFIED AT THE BEGINNING, SEE ASSEMBLY VS COMPONENT CONSIDERATIONS.	REALIZATION THAT UNTIL THEN WE WERE USING THE WRONG LEVERS TO SECURE A SAFE COMPONENT DESIGN.	YES – SEE THE ACTIVITIES: DEFINE COMPONENT ASSUMPTIONS AND DEFINE LEVERS AND SET DOE, DONE UP FRONT Figure 5.13.
5	MASS DISTRIBUTION FOR THE FRAME CALCULATED WITH THE WRONG TYPE OF MATERIAL.	REALIZATION THAT SINCE THE NEW APPROACH STARTED, WE WERE WORKING WITH THE WRONG DESIGN ASSUMPTION INVOLVING THE FRAME MATERIAL.	YES – SEE THE ACTIVITY: DEFINE COMPONENT ASSUMPTIONS, DONE UP FRONT Figure 5.13.
6	USE OF THE ATCH MODEL WITHOUT MAKING SURE IT COVERS THE VARIABILITY.	REALIZATION THAT SINCE THE NEW APPROACH STARTED, WE WERE WORKING WITH A WRONGLY CALIBRATED ATCH MODEL.	YES – SEE THE ACTIVITY VERIFY AND VALIDATE COMPATBILITY OF MODELS, DONE UP FRONT Figure 5.13.
7	CONTINUE TO MODIFY THE FRAME WITH INCOMPLETE CHANGE IMPACT ASSESSMENT.	LATE REALIZATION THAT IT IS TOO COSTLY TO MODIFY THE FRAME.	YES – SEE THE ACTIVITIES: DEFINE COMPONENT ASSUMPTIONS AND DEFINE LEVERS AND SET DOE, DONE UP FRONT Figure 5.13.
8	THE REQUIREMENTS THAT WERE USED TO START THE MOLD FABRICATION WERE SENT WITHOUT "PASS" FROM ALL THE REQUIRED CASES, BEFORE THE APPROACH WAS RESET TO COVER WORKING WITH THE ASSEMBLY.	REALIZATION THAT THE CORRESPONDING DIMENSIONS OF A SAFE COMPONENT DESIGN REQUIRE SCRAPPING THE CURRENT, VERY EXPENSIVE MOLD THE SUPPLIER WAS MACHINING.	YES – REQUIREMENTS SENT AFTER ALL REQUIRED CASES ARE RUN, SEE ACTIVITY DERIVE REQUIREMENTS FOR SAFE COMPONENT, Figure 5.13.

Appendix F2 Summary Icons Current vs Future State VSM

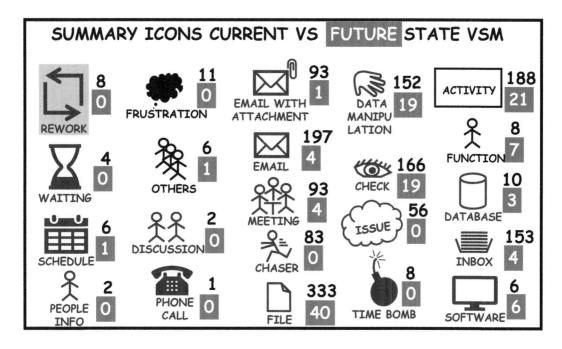

Appendix F3 Summary Table Bursts

Burst	Description	Proposal
A	Dedicated team for 18 weeks, comprising INTG, DSGN, STRU, MECH, THEL, FSAF, CMGT	• the names of the team members, largely being the ones involved in the VSM exercise • a matrix organizational structure where team members will report to the function manager and to the team leader • my name as the team leader, as the INTG function • to keep the same places for now, as the logistics of the move potentially being costly • the new product development VPs name as the approver for organizational change
B	Commitment-based schedule board	• the conference room number that we thought is convenient for all • the name of the INTG team member as the one responsible to design and install the board • the new product development VPs name as the approver of the room being dedicated to the team
C	Daily huddle	• next to the commitment-based board in the proposed conference room • start at 8:00 am for 30 min • the name of the INTG team member to lead the daily huddle • my name to set the objectives and the huddle rules • the request to have a permanent projector in the conference room

Burst	Description	Proposal
D	Standards, knowledge standards	• need a workshop to establish a list of required standards, knowledge standards and the plan to document them – with my name next to it
E	KM tool	• find a temporary solution, more robust than our current eRooms – with my name next to it • work with IT and establish KM tool requirements, find software packages that fit our requirements and install the one that is the most suitable for us – with my name next to it
F	Process for compatibility of models	• workshop to set instructions on how to verify if the models are compatible or not, including decision criteria to identify when and what corrections are necessary – the multifunction team • revise our meshing standard if necessary – the name of the standard owner
G	The DOE process and document	• instructions on how to setup the DOE and how the DOE document looks like, including instructions on how to interpret the results and how to draw conclusions based on the results – the name of the INTG senior specialist
H	The convergence process and document	• instructions on how the convergence is done and how the document looks like, including decision criteria for finding the optimum alternative – the name of the INTG senior specialist
I	Knowledge management system	• make awareness on establishing a company-wide knowledge management system to the company's leadership team – start with the new program development VP – with my name next to it

Appendix F4 Value Stream Improvement Action Plan

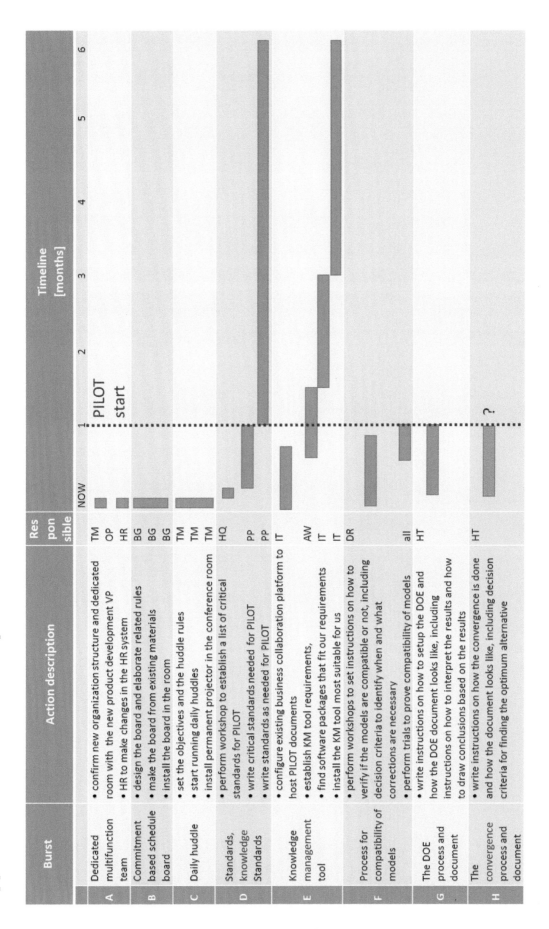

Appendix G: Characters and Stories

Character, story	Context
Denise ***Failed IT solution*** ***implementation*** *Write-off in the books due to underutilization of the IT solution as the result of a failed attempt to integrate the enterprise ERP system with the multi-platform software suite for computer-aided design and with a set of PLM products*	***IT VP, working with Louis for a multinational company that develops and manufactures complicated products. She was involved in VSM before, but in operations; then she saw the results of a successful one in engineering.*** A couple of years ago, the company started a very ambitious IT project called eHOPE with the objective of integrating the enterprise ERP system with the multi-platform software suite for computer-aided design and with a set of PLM products in order to streamline the product development work. It was not a smooth ride. Besides the inherent technical complications, leadership and team member turnaround (Denise and Louis were not part of the original team), the project was haunted by scope changes and overlapping roles and responsibilities. More than a dozen IT, engineering and business functions were involved, like IT project office, data management, process and tools, design engineering, while working with the software provider and the solution architect. One source of frustration along the way was the difference of opinions of the different stakeholders on how to proceed. As stakeholders were defending their particular points of view, progress was slow and misguided, ending with late delivery and user frustration, as the delivered functionality didn't meet their needs.
Louis ***Failed IT solution*** ***implementation***	***Engineering process and tools director, working with Denise for a multinational company that develops and manufactures complicated products. He has not been involved with VSM before.***

Character, story	Context
Claire ***Supplier unpaid invoices*** *Line stop and delayed delivery due to missing parts, as the supplier refuses to ship new parts without being paid*	*Supplier account manager, working in supply chain for another multinational company that uses a sophisticated ERP system. She already participated in a successful VSM exercise involving aftermarket work.* The sophisticated ERP system is used to control production, inventories and accounts payable. This complicated system consists of three integrated main modules: one for finance, one for supply chain and one for production, with user access granted just for the corresponding function. Automated transactions are mixed with manual entries made by hundreds of people for thousands of suppliers. The inherent complications of the system make it such that the main stakeholders have just a partial view – their function's view – on the stream that links ordering a part, receiving the part, receiving the invoice and finally paying the invoice. In order to see what's happening with the unpaid invoices, Claire needs to navigate through several system transactions and scrutinize dozens of system screens and still might not be able to have the whole information. It might take her dozens of email exchanges or phone calls with production and finance people to finally understand what's wrong and why the supplier was not paid.
Ted **Wrong requirements for critical component sent to supplier, new product development** *Program cost overrun and delays due to sending wrong requirements to the supplier for a critical component*	*Engineering director, working with Frank in a complicated new product development program for another multinational company. He previously had bad experiences with VSM, but Frank convinced him to try again.* The inherent complications of the new product make it such that several highly specialized engineering functions are required to interact with each other in order to progress the design, working with hundreds of requirements and design variables. Because they are developing a new product, they are in unexplored territory, dealing with unknowns, making assumptions and forced to go through a lot of iterations to solve the complicated design challenges. For example, one highly specialized engineering function gets data from another function, runs it through a specific model, performs analysis, applies engineering judgment, debugs the model and makes corrections – could be several cycles like this – then hands the resulting engineering data to another function, who then does the same. It goes without saying that this manual process allows for errors to go unnoticed and to propagate in the design. Additionally, people favor the designs that satisfy their narrow functional view, to the detriment of the product's view. In this environment, it is not uncommon to hear comments like, "I don't know what result I'll get, and I don't know when I'll give it to you," or "Our function's portion should be extracted and dealt as separate … this is the only way we will get what our function wants in a reasonable time." Besides dealing with too many design variables, Ted's challenge is amplified by the fact that his team is dependent on all the other functions' work in order to perform properly while having no authority over the others', as they report to their own functional management.

Character, story	Context
Frank **Engineering change process** *Delivery delays and penalties due to long lead times for engineering changes*	*Program director, working with Ted in a complicated new product development program for another multinational company. He already participated in several successful VSM exercises, one for the engineering change process and used this example to convince Ted to try again performing one.*

Index

Note: Page numbers in *italic* indicate a figure and page numbers in **bold** indicate a table on the corresponding page.

For Product Safety Concerns and Information please contact our EU
representative GPSR@taylorandfrancis.com Taylor & Francis Verlag GmbH,
Kaufingerstraße 24, 80331 München, Germany

Printed and bound by CPI Group (UK) Ltd, Croydon, CR0 4YY

01/05/2025

01858590-0001